A Highschool Teacher Goes to War

David Volk

Copyright © 2007 David Volk
All rights reserved.
ISBN: 1-4196-5761-5
ISBN-13: 978-1419657610

Visit www.booksurge.com to order additional copies.

Draftee

DEDICATION: This book is dedicated to the men and women who have served this great country in the armed forces over the years, with special thanks to the 2.5 million who were drafted and served during the Vietnam War Era.

CONTENTS

INTRODUCTION	xi
CHAPTER 1: Basic Training	1
CHAPTER 2: Drill Sergeants	5
CHAPTER 3: Infantry and Rumor of Infantry	17
CHAPTER 4: "Uncle Ben's Rest Home" — Dinfos	23
CHAPTER 5: Preparing For War	33
CHAPTER 6: "And It's One, Two, Three, What Are We Fighting For, Well I Don't Give A Damn, Next Stop Is Vietnam."	37
CHAPTER 7: "Good Morning, Vietnam" — Daily Life in the RVN.	45
CHAPTER 8: "When the Going Gets Weird The Weird Turn Pro."	69
CHAPTER 9: Assorted fruits and Nuts: "Piss Willy" to "Joe the Shit Man."	85
CHAPTER 10: I Don't Mean to Get Off on a Rant Here.	97
CHAPTER 11: "There's No Place Like Home; There's No Place Like Home."	101
EPILOGUE	109

Endorsements

"The Vietnam War, like those of us who participated, varied from year by year, battlefield to battlefield. In the utter insanity and absurdity of those difficult years each of us learned to cope with the terror and boredom that each day presented us, almost always with unbridled, unabashed humor."

"Volk's book is honest and his humor is refreshing. There is also a quiet courage in this story. Very young men, drafted from the craziness of the 60's into the daffiness of military life during war."

Rick Eilert, author, "For Self And Country".

"As someone who lived through these pages, reading this book was like watching an old movie that has been in storage for more than 30 years.

"Volk's keen eye for detail and incredible memory resurrected a rather dismal time with sensitivity, insight and—most of all—a healthy dose of humor."

Sergio Ortiz
Writer-photographer
Combat correspondent in Vietnam for the U.S. Marine Corps

"What was it like for a middle class kid from South Dakota to be drafted and shipped off to Vietnam? In pitch perfect prose, Volk chronicles his incredible journey from average civilian to wartime soldier in "DRAFTEE: A High School Teacher Goes to War.".........Moving, memorable and funny."

New York Times best-selling author Ellen Tanner Marsh

INTRODUCTION

Some time ago, while watching the Super Bowl with friends, a very poignant commercial from Budweiser came on, which showed American GIs coming home from Iraq or Afghanistan. As these soldiers walked through the train or airport terminal, people spontaneously stood and applauded.

One of my friends turned to me and said, "Not quite your homecoming from Vietnam, Dave." My other friends kind of waited for me to say something or relate incidents that I had encountered when I came back in 1970. The only thing I could think, however, was, "Thank God this country has finally got it right. Thank God this country has finally figured out how to send young men and women off to war and welcome them home again—regardless of what the philosophical or political feelings might be with regard to those wars."

The other impact that commercial and exchange with friends had was to motivate me finally to put down on paper some of the experiences I had, the people I met, and the impressions left by serving as a two-year draftee between 1969 and 1971 in the U.S. Army.

It has always seemed to me that the Vietnam War, including its aftereffects, was always framed from the viewpoint of the extremes.

If life does imitate art—and I happen to think it does—then the movies of the time are excellent examples. At one end of the spectrum there were pro-war propaganda films like John Wayne's "Green Berets," and at the other end, anti-war propaganda movies like "Born on the Fourth of July" and Jane Fonda's incredibly dark, dreary, and depressing film "Coming Home."

So I wanted to view this time period from something other then the extremes. I wanted to view it from the perspective of one ordinary soldier who was abruptly drafted, went off to the insane world of basic training, got shipped off to war with all of the accompanying culture shock that involved, and, after suffering a few ill effects on return, readapted and was given a wonderful life with some material successes and, more importantly, a wealth of good friends.

History has always been one of my passions, and I have always lamented that so much history is lost before it can be recorded. The huge events, of course, are covered and re-covered, but the minutiae of everyday life—the small things that make up people's existence day to day—are too soon forgotten.

Anyway, because I did not want to lose that minutiae—the stages, the plots, and the cast of characters of my incredible journey as a soldier—I have decided to try and put it down before time and old age take it out of reach.

This tale will not contain many deep philosophical positions on the "rights" and "wrongs" of the American involvement in Vietnam: the policy of containment, the bombings of the North, the draft, or the treatment of soldiers on their return. I sometimes take some big issues out of the box when they apply to the experiences that my fellow soldiers and I had during this strange time in American history. The Vietnam War itself has been debated and dissected enough.

I will take some pokes at officers and senior NCOs; however, that is to be expected since a two-year draftee is telling this tale. Since the dawn of time, when one cave man decided to put on a saber-tooth necklace and call himself the leader, ordinary soldiers have not felt very kindly toward officers or senior NCOs.

First, a short personal history.

I was born in 1947 in Mitchell, South Dakota, and grew up in what has to have been the best time ever to be a young boy in America. My life revolved around two loving parents, four brothers of varying ages, and an assortment of different small town neighborhoods full of wonderful friends and adventure. This was a time for family, when mothers stayed home and took care of virtually everything, including all the other kids in the neighborhood. It was a time for community, when Mrs. Ayres down the street told you to stop spraying girls with the hose, and her admonition was taken just as seriously as if it had come from your own mom.

It was a time when, on a Saturday morning after chores, I got on my bike and left for the day to go fishing, play pick-up baseball, or just shoot the breeze with buddies.

It truly was a simpler and more innocent time. Take sex education for an example. Today it seems like a very complicated and controversial issue; however, when I grew up it had just three simple components:

1. School: Since I went to a Catholic school sex education involved a twenty-minute class in junior high. A priest talked to the boys and a nun to the girls. This lecture essentially covered rudimentary information on human anatomy, and the differences between little boys and little girls.

2. My father: When I asked him where babies came from he gave me an earnest look and explained that an angel came down and planted a seed in the mommy that grew into a baby. Years later, after I had been married for quite awhile, he asked when Susan and I were going to start a family. I replied that I was just waiting for the angel to plant the seed.

3. Buddies: Here was the real source of knowledge for all things sexual. I vividly remember my first introduction to a topic involving that mystery of mysteries...SEX! Some pals and I were sprawled out under a tree one hot summer morning after a baseball game and one of the brighter members of my group was telling us about, what in those days, was called a rubber.

I was fascinated as this sexual genius told us that he not only knew what a rubber was but that he had actually seen one. According to him it was a rubber hose type of a device, which was closed and rounded at one end and this was fit over your "pecker" (our word of choice back then for describing the male member). This hose was then attached to a jock strap type of apparatus that you wore.

Now, why anyone would want or need such a thing wasn't quite clear to me as my sex education did not follow a natural progression and the whole subject of the actual sex act had not been covered yet.

I almost feel sorry for young people today in their over-scheduled, over-organized, over-indulged world. The unimaginable joy of being young and free is something that they will never understand or know, and I think that is too bad.

Anyway, it was a wonderful life that continued on through high school and into college. At Northern State College in Aberdeen, South Dakota, I got my first political break and went to work as field representative for U.S. Congressman Ben Reifel. I would hold that job right up until I was drafted.

1969

1969 was one of those watershed years for me, which people have throughout their lives. In a somewhat chronological order, this was the year:

1. A good friend—39-year-old Frank Farrar—had just been elected governor, and a number of my other friends were going to Pierre with him. My first love has always been politics, and I looked forward to the opportunity to get involved somehow with the new administration.
2. I was going to get married that spring to a wonderful woman.
3. I was going to graduate from college at the end of summer.
4. I still had my own office in downtown Aberdeen, from which I ran Congressman Reifel's field office.
5. I was the only teacher in my graduating class to sign a teaching contract with a Class A school (a designation for the state's largest districts that included my anticipated destination, Pierre). My wife-to-be was also signing a contract with that school district.

6. As the summer started, my new wife and I found a house to rent in Pierre for almost nothing, as the guy just wanted someone to look after it.
7. Both my wife and I had just bought new cars.
8. Man would first walk on the moon.
9. Hell, to show you what a crazy year it would be, the Mets would even win the World Series.

In other words, ladies and gentlemen, I had it made. That is, until sometime that summer a letter arrived, which I believe started, "Your friends and neighbors have selected you for induction into the U.S. Army." *My friends and neighbors!!!* What the hell kind of friends or neighbors do that?

So, instead of heading to Pierre to teach and find political glory, with my new wife and new car, I was headed for the army three days after I graduated from college.

CHAPTER 1

BASIC TRAINING

My college graduation ceremony, army physical, and trip to beautiful Fort Lewis, Washington, are all somewhat hazy. One thing, however, does stick out from my physical in Sioux Falls, South Dakota. I went over with some friends who were also being drafted, and while we were sitting around in our underwear, in walked another guy who had to be 6'4", 220 pounds of rawboned South Dakota farm boy muscle. Behind him walked a guy 5'3", 120 pounds, soaking wet, with a fairly pronounced cleft palate. By now you are way ahead of me, as the farm boy was declared 4-F (unfit for military service) and sent back to somewhere in western South Dakota, where he would throw 800-pound hay bales around for the rest of his life, and Don Knotts with a hare lip was going into the army. It was my first of many Wizard-of-Oz, "Toto, I have a feeling we're not in Kansas anymore" flashes that I would have during my military career.

My most vivid memories of the induction center at Fort Lewis are a lot of yelling, dire threats about drugs and contraband, and some cheery news about how a lot of us would either get killed or badly mangled in Vietnam.

To make matters worse, back in Sioux Falls after our physicals, my buddies and I had about four hours to kill before our plane left. We promptly found a bar called Ed Slears. Showing up for the army with a hangover is a bad idea.

"HELL, THIS ISN'T GOING TO BE SO BAD"

The next few days were a blur of getting more physicals, shots, uniforms, and so on. Finally, I was put with a group of other trainees who would proudly make up B-5-2 Basic Training Company.

Now, in my brief autobiography, I described my "Beaver Cleaver" upbringing in the bosom of the white Anglo-Saxon Midwest. With that as a background, imagine my thoughts as I looked around the group at blacks with Afros as big as beach balls, Chicanos with waves of oily hair swept back in nasty-looking duck butts, longhaired weirdo white guys from California who all looked like Charles Manson wannabes.

I finally spotted someone with short hair and a semblance of intelligence in his panic-stricken eyes and went over to introduce myself. He turned out to be a great guy from Oregon, who was also having some trouble with the appearance of some our fellow B-5-2ers. I finally said, "Killed in Vietnam? Hell, we will never make it out of basic training."

There is a lot the army did during the short time I was a soldier that I never understood. The "shearing of the sheep" for basic training, however, is brilliant.

In a matter of minutes, some of the scariest people I had ever seen were transformed into meek and mild-looking GIs. I swear, you take four pounds of grease-laden hair off a small Mexican-American kid, and it is a transformation.

Now, understand that there were still some fairly strange guys in this outfit. Back in 1969, there was a program that essentially allowed a lot of young lawbreakers to go to the U.S. Army rather than jail, and I had a sense that this rule probably applied to a good many boys of B-5-2. They sure as hell didn't look as tough, though, with all their hair on the floor. By the way, after my haircut my looks did not change much, except perhaps to make me look even more like a dork. I am sure no one thought, "Damn, that tall, skinny, white kid with the black horn-rimmed glasses isn't nearly so scary now that he has his hair cut."

During this time of getting processed and inducted, we were

shepherded around by some Specialist Fours, who yelled once in a while but essentially said things like: "This way, gentlemen, get in line here, people, move over to the mess, guys." Hardly the stuff of Jack Webb in the movie "DI." So one day after getting situated in our barracks, we were sitting around outside smoking, and the words, "Hell, this isn't going to be so bad" were barely out of my mouth when I saw four guys of varying shapes and colors wearing Smokey Bear hats headed our way.

The fury with which they tore into us is indescribable. They were like ravenous wolves among a flock of newly shorn lambs. The swearing, yelling, grabbing, and shoving were something to behold. They finally got us into something resembling a formation, and as I was standing there in sheer terror, one of our previous gentle shepherds walked by. I whispered out of the side of my mouth, "Who are those guys?" As he walked off, he replied, "Those are your drill sergeants. Welcome to the army, soldier."

CHAPTER 2

DRILL SERGEANTS

It is difficult to describe drill sergeants if you have never been in the army. I suppose the first thing you notice about them is their incredible command of the English language. They could scream one sentence that would go on for two minutes, and it would make perfect sense in a profane sort of way. They worked with curse words like a poet works with free verse or rhyme.

The first couple of days were by far the worst with these hounds from hell. One of the exercises they put us through was a procedure called a "footlocker drill," whereby all fifty-three of us in B-5-2 would rush into our barracks, grab our footlockers, and then rush outside again to get into formation. Then repeat it. I lost count how many times we did this. Obviously the last ones out were additionally punished, so this truly turned into what the army lovingly calls a "cluster fuck."

I remember the first night in our barracks after being introduced to our drill sergeants. We all lay dead tired after a day of being screamed at, bullied, abused, and run ragged. The place was dead silent when one weary member of our group piped up and said, "I's got to call my congressman and have him get me out of this hellhole." The place erupted with laughter. I never even knew who said it, but he gave us all a gift that night.

Before I go on about drill sergeants, let me comment on our barracks. We had been in temporary housing until we got hooked up with our drill sergeants, but now we were in what would be our home for the next nine weeks. The best way to describe Fort Lewis barracks is to say: think World War II and every movie you ever saw about soldiers getting ready to go fight the "Big One." Wooden, two-story structures with linoleum floors. Ten or so bunk beds down each side with footlockers against the wall. Two small private rooms at the front, which were reserved for the platoon guide and squad leaders. Latrines in the back. The middle of the barracks floor between the bunks belonged to the drill sergeant, and you did not walk on it, even in your stocking feet.

Because the barracks had been built almost a quarter of a century earlier and were made of wood, the drill sergeants explained to us that if they caught fire, they would burn completely to the ground in about three minutes. There were water-filled butt cans attached to every support post in the place, and a nasty job called "Fire Guard," whereby all night long recruits on two-man, two-hour shifts would walk around constantly making sure there wasn't a fire.

Later, when I became a squad leader, I was relieved of this onerous duty and simply made out the roster for the night, which in itself was a handy disciplinary device as the 3:00 a.m. to 5:00 a.m. shift was a bitch. Once, while getting up to take a leak, I checked on my ever-vigilant fireguard and not only found him asleep, but with a still-smoldering cigarette in his hand. While my army skills were not that well honed, even I could tell this was probably not a good thing and explained to him that sleeping was bad enough, but sleeping with a lit cig would not be tolerated. General Patton I was not.

One break I did get in basic is that I drew someone named Sergeant First Class Storey as my platoon drill sergeant. Of all our drill instructors, he was the only one who seemed to have any appreciation for someone's intelligence and maturity. It seemed the other drill sergeants selected their squad leaders and platoon guide based on how big or mean they were, but not Storey.

After a time he was to become a mentor to me; however, even from the start he tried to help me adjust to this alien world. His best advice: "Volk, keep your sense of humor."

Quite frankly, considering how these sergeants talked, there was not much danger of that, because when they were not scaring the hell out of me they cracked me up. This one time we were given some rather old equipment, and Sergeant Storey said, "Shit, we've had this stuff since Christ was a corporal in the Jewish National Guard."

Drill sergeants almost never used someone's actual name. What they would do was take whatever distinguished you from the others and use that name followed by the word "fuck." For example, because of my Buddy Holly-style glasses, I was a "four-eyed fuck." A heavy person was a "fat fuck," a slim person a "skinny fuck," a lazy person or complainer a "malingering fuck," and so on.

This practice led to truly one of the funniest things I have ever encountered. To this day I have no understanding why I thought it was funny at the time, or why I still find it hilarious.

We were all standing in the rain during mail call. When your name was called, you yelled, "YES, DRILL SERGEANT!" and double-timed up to get your mail, then returned to your place in formation. Anyway, I heard Gonzales' name called. Now Gonzales, who was in my squad and who was missing two or three of his front teeth, did not answer, although I knew he was there. Sergeant Storey called his name again, and still no answer; so I looked around, and there stood Gonzales, in a puddle of water up to his ankles, looking like the saddest sack in the army. Physically he was still in Fort Lewis, but mentally he was back in his small New Mexico town, cruising for chicks in his '56 Chevy.

Sarge by this time had had it, and screamed, "Gonzales, you toothless fuck, get up here!" Well, I lost it. I doubled over with laughter and could not regain control. Storey, who did not like to discipline his squad leaders in front of the troops, whispered ominously, "Square yourself away, squad leader," but I was gone. Someone sticking an M16 in my left ear and threatening to pull the trigger would have only induced more laughter. I soon found myself facedown in the wet gravel, but it was worth every push-up. I guess Sergeant Storey's advice to "keep my sense of humor" had its limits. (I need to add something here about the weather at Ft. Lewis, Washington. While I am sure the sun does shine on Seattle once in awhile I don't remember seeing it during my basic training. There was a popular song out at that time by Perry Como called "Seattle". One of the lines goes "The bluest skies you've ever seen are in Seattle". There was a guy from Seattle in our company and every time that song would play everyone would find something to throw at the poor SOB.)

As I said, to this day I cannot explain why I have found this so funny, but it was a tonic back then and still is today. So God bless you, Gonzales. I hope you came out of the army in good shape, got your teeth fixed, and are still cruising for chicks in New Mexico.

When I write down the incredible language of these drill sergeants, it sounds coarse even by today's standards, where any episode of "Deadwood" on HBO contains the word "fuck" a hundred times in an evening. Back then, however, it became totally natural and expected, and if I think real hard I can recall today some of that long ago litany of profanity:

"YOU MAGGOT!!! YOU FUCKING MAGGOT!!!! I'M GOING TO KILL YOU!!!!! I'M GOING TO RIP OUT YOUR FUCKING EYES AND SKULL — FUCK YOU TO DEATH!!!!"

I mean it. These guys were good.

You literally could get yelled at just by standing on a sidewalk. Once I was standing around the barracks and did not see a drill sergeant coming up behind me until I heard him yell, "Make a hole, whore!!!"

To this day, whenever I get together with some of my army buddies, I will walk up behind one of them and say, "Make a hole, whore." It never fails to get us laughing. Some things truly are timeless.

In addition to constantly being verbally abused, there were other ways that they reminded us of our standing on the ladder of importance in the U.S. Army. Most visible was a white patch, emblazoned with our unit that was worn above our name. It was aptly called a "maggot patch." I still have mine.

BECOMING A SOLDIER

In addition to showing up for the army with a hangover, I also showed up with a badly scraped left palm. I had acquired this non-combat wound a number of days earlier at my college graduation, when after thanking our parents and sending them on their way, some friends and I proceeded to celebrate our lofty accomplishment of a college degree.

My best friend, Chuck Strasburg, and I were in the parking lot of the local Holiday Inn, arms draped over each other and singing our hearts out, when Chuck stumbled, pulling us both to the graveled lot. I immediately put out my left hand to break my fall and left most of my palm skin on the ground. (It should be noted here that for the last thirty-five years, Strasburg has claimed that it was I who caused the fall, but he was a Democrat back in college and a notorious liar.)

Regardless of fault, I was leaving in two days for the land of the perpetual push-up, chin-up, and dreaded parallel bars with a badly skinned left palm.

One of the first things you are subject to at basic training is a Physical Test (PT), a series of obstacles, exercises, running, and so on. The army does this early so they have some idea just how badly out of shape the new recruits are. I was fine with everything, even push-ups and chin-ups, as I could adjust how I used my left hand. The parallel bars were another story. Parallel bars are nothing more than the evenly spaced bar rungs that you see on every playground. You have to move down these bars hand over hand until the end. I didn't make it halfway.

Now the obvious question here is why didn't I just go to the drill sergeant and explain my injury and get excused. Very early on, I had noticed how well drill sergeants received complaints, excuses, and alibis, and while "four-eyed fuck" wasn't the greatest moniker, exchanging it for "malingering fuck" did not seem like a career move I wanted to make.

The result of all this was that, on a sunny Saturday morning, the first time we were actually given some free time in the barracks and allowed to turn on radios, I found myself in a formation with a sorry collection of fatties, mama's boys, limp-wristed half steppers, 90-pound weaklings, and the like. Our job—retake the PT test.

Oh, how the mighty had fallen. Just two weeks earlier, I had worked for a United States Congressman, was respected in the business and political community of Aberdeen, South Dakota, had just married a great young woman, was getting ready to start a career in teaching, and my political future stretched out before me. Now there I was, in Fort Lewis, Washington, among the, weak, lame, and unmotivated, about to retake the PT test while friends back in the barracks enjoyed free time and rock and roll.

That was the nadir of my army life. As strange as it sounds, and considering everything I would experience in Vietnam, it was the closest I ever came to going AWOL during my army career. I have no idea what I would have done if I actually could have gotten off the base and gone AWOL, although I am quite sure it would have involved tracking down Charlie Strasburg and beating the shit out of him.

I finally did explain my situation to Sergeant Storey, and he did substitute something for the parallel bars until I healed. To this day, I am always amazed at the depth of my depression over something that now seems so trivial.

It was shortly after this that the draft lottery came out. We all looked to see where we would have been, and while I don't remember how the lottery worked, I do remember that my birth date and letter of my last name were dead last. In other words, women and the furniture would have been drafted before me. And the hits just kept on coming.

When you think about it, army life for a two-year draftee back in 1969 was very much like going to prison. You were dragged off against your will to a place you didn't want to go to and not allowed to leave when you wanted to (which was about two minutes after my arrival). You were told when to eat, go to the bathroom, smoke, use the phone, and obviously there was nothing that resembled either women or booze. And like prison, the whole damn experience was both scary and dangerous.

I remember one Sunday afternoon when the squad leaders got to go over to the main post unsupervised. It was bliss: pizza, beer, and total freedom to use a phone without a line of guys outside the booth yelling for you to hurry up.

Phone privileges were strictly controlled in basic and permitted for a short time at the end of the day. If you were not among the first in line, you were SOL (Shit Out of Luck).

I remember one time a trainee pleading with the drill sergeant to use the phone outside of the regular phone schedule. Apparently he was having problems with his wife. The drill sergeant compassionately replied, "Goddamit, trainee, if the army had wanted you to have a fucking wife, it would have issued you one."

TRAINEES I REMEMBER:

One of most tenacious and determined guys in our company was also our worst soldier. I have no idea what his name was, as the drill sergeants simply referred to him as "you malingering fuck," and I nicknamed him the Hunchback of Fort Lewis, or Hunch for short.

This guy had passed all of his induction physicals, but somehow, at the beginning of basic, had mysteriously developed some terrible back problem, which caused him to walk all hunched over. No medical testing could find anything wrong with Hunch, and for the few weeks he was with us his life was a living hell. Discovering phantom ailments is not something the army takes lightly.

No amount of abuse, humiliation, KP, or derision from his fellow soldiers could cure Hunch of his bad back and his bent-over posture. The rest of us always speculated that when the army finally relented and gave him his medical discharge, old Hunch would stand up straight, snap off a smart salute, and skip out of the building. By the way, he got his discharge—less then honorable, I am sure—and is probably in Hollywood today, as he was one helluva character actor.

The other thing I remember about him is that he was one of the greatest and most ardent cigarette smokers I have ever met. If he didn't have a cigarette, he would come up to you with these pitiful, pleading eyes and beg for a drag, and he was always fishing butts out of the gutter. "Police call," where we would line up and pick up trash and cigarette butts, was a pain in the ass for everyone but Hunch. First off, he was all bent over and could see the ground well, and most importantly it always provided him with a new cache of semi-smoked cigarettes.

Another guy I remember from our company was named Melvin Laird, which at that time was the same name as the then U.S. Secretary of Defense. Now, our Laird was a bit of a screw-up, and I remember one time the drill sergeant screaming at him, "Laird, is your father that asshole in Washington?"

Laird yelled back, "No, Drill Sergeant!"

The sarge yelled again, "Are you sure your father is not that asshole in Washington?"

"Yes, Drill Sergeant," yelled Laird

"What does your father do, Laird?"

"He's dead, Drill Sergeant."

"Well, good, that's very good, Laird, because your ass is mine."

As far as self-disciplining that you hear about or see in movies, I did not see a great deal of it at Fort Lewis. There were times when the whole company was made to do push-ups while the screw-up got to stand and do nothing. I do not, however, remember a lot of that.

I did see a trainee walk out of a formation once, and the drill sergeants turned their backs while five guys from the platoon went and rather roughly dragged him back to the formation.

I am aware of only one blanket party in my platoon (a blanket party being where a blanket is thrown over the malingerer and everyone takes turns punching him). I did not take part, however, as I was a squad leader and as such represented the drill sergeant in the barracks—and of course the U.S. Army did not sanction these type of rituals.

KP

I had to pull KP (Kitchen Police) only once during basic, because once I made squad leader I was exempt. That one time was enough.

Truly the meanest people in the U.S. Army are the guys who run mess halls. I swear to God, if this would have been 1943 and these cooks would have been in the German Wehrmacht, they would have all been SS guards at a concentration camp.

One particularly nasty fat slob sat around all day yelling, "I haven't smacked me a goddamn meat"—that being us—"all day."

Our day started before dawn and ended way after dark. We got ten minutes to eat breakfast, lunch, and dinner (after everyone else had been served), and we got a fifteen-minute smoke break in the afternoon. I also was given the honor of cleaning the grease trap, which has to be one of the most truly disgusting jobs on the planet. It was the longest day of my life. When we got back to the barracks—smelly, greasy, and bone-tired—we discovered that the rest of the company had been allowed to go over to the PX to buy toothpaste, shaving cream, etc. The day had just gotten worse.

MARCHING

Obviously, learning to march is job one in basic training, and quite frankly it wasn't something I was very good at initially. I have never been the coordinated type, and while marching looks easy, it helps to have some sense of rhythm and coordination. Not me.

I have always envied my male friends who could dance, as dancing always seemed like a sure-fire way to meet women. The truth is, if I would have had to rely on my dancing ability to score with women, I would still be a virgin.

I wish I could remember better some of the wonderful

marching cadences the drill sergeants would sing. Like their cursing, some of it was truly inspired.

There were, of course, the old standbys:

"Ain't no use of looking down, ain't no discharge on the ground."

"Ain't no use of looking back, Jody's got your Cadillac."

"Ain't no use of goin' home, Jody got your girl and gone."

"Jody," by the way, was the name given to the 4-F bastard who was back home screwing your wife, girlfriend, and sister.

I have never met many male Jodys in my life, but I've never trusted a one of them.

"I want to be an Airborne Ranger, I want to live a life of danger, I want to go to Vietnam, I want to kill old Charlie Cong." I'll sing it, Sarge, but I won't believe it.

Interestingly enough, less than a year later I would spend almost a month with the Airborne Rangers of the 101st Airborne Division in Vietnam.

Ultimately, marching was something I learned to do quite well, as did our entire company. In fact, one of those rare times — when everything seems just right and you feel at harmony with everything around you — happened while I was marching at Fort Lewis, Washington, during basic training.

It was toward the end of our training, and we were coming back to the barracks at sunset on a beautiful fall day. Instead of the usual marching songs and cadence about "Going to Vietnam and killing ol' Charlie Cong," we sang a soft, beautiful ballad that partly went, "Around her neck she wore a silver locket; she wore it for her true love who was far, far away. Far away, far away, she wore it for her true love who was far, far away."

I know this sounds sappy, and I am probably not explaining it very well, but as I said, it was one of those rare times when you are right where you should be, with the exact people you should be with. Somehow this ragtag conglomeration of blacks, Mexican-Americans, California hippies, and one Midwest tight-ass Republican had come together as an actual army unit. What made it even stranger was that just a few weeks before I had felt like someone had dropped me off on Mars.

I cared about these guys. Hell, to the men in my squad I was not only one of them, I was their leader. Due to my advanced age (twenty-two) and education (college degree), I was also their advisor and confidant. I was "The Professor." They were my guys, and we depended on each other.

Somehow, in some strange way, I had unwittingly become a soldier. Not a great Sergeant York or Audie Murphy-type soldier, but a soldier nonetheless.

CHAPTER 3

INFANTRY AND RUMOR OF INFANTRY.

There is an old maxim that an army travels on its stomach. I don't know about that, as we always had plenty to eat. Not great food, mind you, but always enough. (To this day, I cannot stand to be in the same room with liver and onions, after a nasty encounter with that particular dish in basic.)

There is another adage that an army also travels on rumors, and that one is true. We were constantly hearing, "The war is ending," or "There is a shortage of officers, and some us are going to Officer Candidate School (OCS)," and even,

"Guys on their way to Vietnam are miraculously pulled off their plane at the stopover in Hawaii, and then spend the rest of their tour as lifeguards on Waikiki Beach for nurses." I always liked that one, and waited expectantly in Honolulu on my way to Vietnam.

Quite frankly, I never paid much attention to these until I heard a particularly vicious rumor that college graduates were the best candidates to be sent across a parade ground at Fort Lewis and become the worst thing that could happen to an army trainee: 11 Bravo—Advanced Infantry Training, and a sure-fire ticket to the jungles of Vietnam.

Now, as a two-year draftee, I never expected that the army would make me a general. I always figured, however, that with my education and the fact that I could type they would certainly find something better for me than becoming cannon fodder for the infantry.

By this time, I had a pretty relaxed relationship with Sergeant Storey, so I took this rumor to him, fully expecting him to dispel it and assure me that I would be safely sent off to "Clerk Jerk" training somewhere. Not so.

Now, before I relate what Storey told me, I need to introduce one more person from my company: Peter Wong. Without a doubt, the dumbest trainee in North America. I don't mean that cruelly; he was just dumb. I'm talking houseplant dumb. Of course, within minutes of being in the army, he was nicknamed "Wong Peter"—something his parents should have thought about before naming him.

Anyway, Storey looked at me and said, "No, that's right, a lot of college grads are sent to 11 Bravo. Think about it, Volk." Then he nodded over to Peter Wong, who was trying to master the intricacies of lacing and tying his boots. "If you are in the jungle and your life might depend on the guy to your left or right, do you want one of those guys to be Wong Peter?"

It was as if someone suddenly hit me in the stomach. How could this be? How could all the things I had done right, like getting a college education, now conspire to have my sorry ass dragged across that parade ground to 11 Bravo and certain death in Vietnam?

"Toto, I have a feeling we're not in Kansas anymore."

At about the same time, a guy from California mentioned another interesting rumor. It involved an MOS (Military Occupational Specialty) called White House Communications. This job involved being either in the White House or in one of Nixon's headquarters at either Key Biscayne or San Clemente.

Now, the California guy who had heard about this MOS was not a good candidate for a job in White House Communications. Back before we were given our GI haircut, he was the guy who looked like Charles Manson, and I have a sense that by 1969 he had probably smoked more pot than the entire state of South Dakota.

I, however—a life-long, tight-ass Young Republican, who had worked for a U.S. Congressman—was a perfect candidate. The words of that unknown trainee that first night in our barracks hauntingly returned: "I's got to call my congressman and have him get me out of this hellhole."

Now, it had become known that I used to work for a congressman. That was partly my doing, as my friends on Congressman Reifel's staff had asked if they could do anything for me, and I told them just to drop an envelope in the mail a couple of times a week with the congressman's name on it—which they did. So twice a week or so I would get this mail from a congressional office, and this practice finally got me called into the commander's office.

It should be remembered that this was an incredibly political war, with a good deal of political interference. Once when I was in the mess hall, my drill sergeant called me back to where he was seated with some other drill sergeants. He said, "Volk, tell them who you used to work for," and I replied, "A U.S. Congressman, Drill Sergeant." One of his buddies then said, "Fuck, we're all going to jail."

All of this congressional attention to "Maggot" trainee Volk finally got me called into the commander's office.

We had little to do with officers in basic. Our first commander was a 2nd lieutenant (Butter Bar) and reminded me a lot of Lieutenant Fuzz in Beetle Bailey. Our second commander, with whom I would meet, was a morose, dark type who I thought acted a lot like Captain Queeg in "The Caine Mutiny." The only thing missing were the steel balls in the palm of his hand and a babbling monologue about catching the guys who had stolen the strawberries.

When I reported to him, he was looking at some papers and did not look up. He simply said, "You having problems, Volk?" I said no, so he wanted to know about all this mail from my congressman, still not looking up. I told him that I had worked for the congressman, and these were letters from him and his staff.

He finally, slowly, looked up at me, as if I were a dangerous virus that was going to keep him from becoming the next five-star General of the Army.

I had no intention of causing any problems for anyone at Fort Lewis. My only concern was getting my D.C. friends to investigate an MOS called White House Communication. A straw was flying by in the tornado and I was grabbing with everything I had. The alternative was 11 Bravo and a date with the NVA.

If you had enlisted for a three-year tour with the army, you were almost certain to get the MOS you wanted. For two-year draftees like me, however, you were at the mercy of the Green Machine. Again, for reasons mentioned above, I figured I would be spared the infantry.

I cannot describe the fear and dread that I felt waiting for my orders.

However, the day finally arrived when our orders were read, and my name was called for an MOS of 71Q, stationed at Fort Benjamin Harrison in Indiana. Not even the drill sergeants knew what the hell 71Q was; however, one of them did know that the huge army finance center was at Fort Benjamin Harrison.

"You'll be fucking up our paychecks in a couple of months, Volk," he said. To which I thought, "Yah, fucking up paychecks! I can do that! I can do that—no sweat!" In fact, if I could somehow figure out a way to fuck up the paychecks of those Nazi bastards who ran the mess hall, it would be even better.

All I knew was that I was not taking that long walk across the parade ground to the infantry.

The day of leaving basic training finally came, and I packed my duffle bag and was waiting for a bus when I saw some of my friends, who had not been as fortunate. We said our goodbyes. We promised that we would stay in touch, but I think we all knew it was a lie. The thing that had banded us together was the shared misery and experience of basic training. Now I was off to a place that some of the drill sergeants referred to as "Uncle Ben's Rest Home," supposedly to fuck up paychecks, and they were going to walk across the parade field for Advanced Infantry Training.

As I headed off to the auditorium, where I would be processed out of Fort Lewis and get my travel orders, bittersweet was also the order of the day.

Now I was, of course, still under the impression that I was headed off to the Military Finance School, whence I would wreak havoc with the United States Army's payroll system. Havoc was what I probably would have done had I gotten into finance school. I have never been very good with numbers, math, or finances. Even though I would later spend seventeen years as South Dakota's state treasurer, to this day I cannot balance my own checkbook. Sometimes I have become so hopelessly lost with a checkbook balance I have closed a checking account and opened a new one so I could start fresh.

As I sat in this large auditorium, waiting as usual for someone to tell me what to do, I heard a guy in the row ahead of me mention 71Q. I asked him what that was, and he replied that it was DINFOS (Defense Information School) and it was for training information personnel for the army. I was still a little lost, so he somewhat testily explained that it was for army reporters and photographers. "The army has its own reporters?" I thought.

Anyway, he said that was where he was headed, and I said, "Hey, me too." Now this guy gets a real strange look on his face and says, "How in the hell can you be going to DINFOS if you don't even know what it is? I had to sign up for three years, and then they wouldn't even guarantee it."

The guy turned out to be Keith Harmon—a great guy from California who remains my friend to this day—but on that long-ago day back in Fort Lewis he was none too pleased that a two-year draftee like me had gotten the same MOS that had taken him three years to receive.

Now, I have often wondered how such a great MOS like 71Q came my way. I am sure that to the casual observer it might be concluded that my congressional contacts pulled the strings; however, I have never for a minute thought that.

First off, Congressman Ben Reifel was perhaps one of the most principled and scrupulous people I have ever met in politics, and while he might open a door like White House Communication and see if I could get through it, he would never actually put the "fix" in. Secondly, even if he had not been such an honest and fair man, the political danger of helping a former staffer avoid the infantry, whereby someone else's mother's son would have to go, would have been just too great.

No, I think if there was anything at work here besides just dumb luck, it was probably Sergeant Storey. As I mentioned, he had become a mentor and somewhat of a friend; plus, he would have had the means. In spite of what general's think, our army and all the armies through time are run by non-commissioned officers. They know the army, who pushes the right buttons, and how to get things done. When I was getting ready to leave Vietnam in January of 1971 and still had some time left on my two years, I told an E-7 sergeant friend how I hated the thought of getting sent to some cold weather fort for the last months of my army career. He mentioned that he knew the woman who made all the assignments for 6th Army in California, and faster than you could say La-la Land, I was tucked away in a nice little NIKE missile base in the San Fernando Valley.

Back in Fort Lewis, however, I could have cared less how this had happened. I was leaving this place and on my way to a delightfully unmilitary-sounding school called DINFOS. Next stop: "Uncle Ben's Rest Home."

CHAPTER 4

"UNCLE BEN'S REST HOME" — DINFOS.

It is difficult to describe Fort Benjamin Harrison, Indiana, after nine weeks at Fort Lewis, Washington. If there was a tree or a patch of grass anywhere on Fort Lewis, I never saw it. Fort Ben? It looked every bit like a nice college campus. Trees, grassy commons, a small brook running through it, and, best of all, dormitories, not barracks.

We arrived on a Saturday afternoon and checked into our dorm. After nine weeks of basic and being told when you could take a leak, go to eat, use the phone, etc., we now didn't know what to do because there didn't seem to be anyone around who was in charge and who would tell us what to do next. Finally, I saw some old guy in a ski sweater, doing odd jobs and looking like an oddly dressed maintenance worker.

I finally went up to ski sweater and said, "Who the hell is in charge around this place?" To which he replied, "I guess I am. I'm Staff Sergeant Dardin." I was shocked! First day at Fort Ben and I had just gone up and smarted off to a sergeant; this was not starting well.

(This Sergeant Dardin would later become a kind of mascot for my DINFOs class. He was a lovable old army drunk who partied with us throughout our stay. When some of the guys in my class put together a very bad rock band, one of their best songs was "Sergeant Dardin's Lonely Hearts Club Band," and no one loved it more than Sergeant Dardin.)

I indicated to Sergeant Dardin that we had just checked in and didn't know what to do. To which he replied that we were on our own until Monday morning! "Come again, Sarge. We are on our own for the next two days?"

Thirty seconds later we were on a bus to Indianapolis, singing Hank Williams Jr.'s classic, "It's Saturday Night and I Just Paid" at the top of our lungs.

Our first stop in the city was a USO affair at a downtown YMCA. I would imagine someone at the base had told us about this affair. Once again, it was right out of World War II. Young ladies all very properly dressed and chaperoned to within an inch of their lives. I might be confusing this with some movies, but it seemed they were all wearing white gloves.

When I observed the eagle-eyed older women chaperones, I had a flashback to high school and my beloved Order of the Presentation of the Blessed Virgin Mary nuns, who patrolled dances like prison guards, constantly on the lookout for the slightest sign of anything sexual among their hormonally-wracked charges.

After nine weeks of basic, our taste in women was definitely running more to Marilyn Chambers than Mary Poppins, so after some sugary punch, stale cookies, and girls fused to chaperones we were off — next stop strip joints and some good, old-fashioned Saturday night sinning.

I must admit that night is a little blurry. After weeks of no alcohol, our tolerance for booze was probably not very good.

Downtown Indy back in those days was a dive of a place, and the next thing I remember was waking up in a seedy old hotel with a glorious hangover.

Regardless of how I felt on that long ago Sunday, the most important thing was: I was free again!

SCHOOL

DINFOS truly did have to be the wackiest military installation in America.

My God, they had an F Troop! (For those who don't remember, there was a great old TV series in the 1960s called

"F Troop" about a totally screwed-up cavalry fort in the Old West.) Anyway, this F Troop was for the finance school, and these were the guys who would be "fucking up our paychecks in a few months."

Our first sergeant was a huge black man who absolutely was one of the most jovial and kindhearted senior NCOs I would meet in the army. (Now, for those who have served in the army, you know how incredible this is, since, next to army cooks, top sergeants were generally some of the meanest people in the army. I'm talking junkyard dog mean.)

The only thing this first sergeant ever complained to us about is that just once he wished his outfit could win the "top marching" unit award during military events. He would say, "I've looked at your records, and you guys are some of the smartest guys in the army, so can you tell me why I can't win the best marching flag just once?"

We never had a marching competition while I was at Harrison, but I sure hope good old Top won his flag.

Because we were a defense school we had all the services in our school: "Flaps" (Air Force), "Squids" (Navy), "Jar Heads" (Marines), and all the associated women's services. Maybe this was why this place was so strange.

The "Gung Ho" Marine Corps were so afraid that their junior "Jar Heads" at the school would become infected by the rest of us slackers that every once in a while they would send around a nasty-looking gunnery sergeant to "de-slacker" them.

Another thing that distinguished this camp from Lewis was a total lack of the attitude that "If the army wanted you to have a fucking wife, it would have issued you one," and even lowly privates like me could have their wives join them while at school.

So my bride of six months packed up her 1969 Kelly green Camaro with as much household goods as she could, including somehow an ironing board, and headed east. I found and rented a small house, which was approximately six hundred square feet in total size.

In spite of its size, we filled that little house with the wonderful aromas of our first Thanksgiving together, the laughter of many great friends, and the creaking of an old rented bed. Looking back, it was probably some of the happiest days we had while married.

As I mentioned previously, I am still close to some of those friends I made at Harrison: Keith Harmon, Dan Suderman and his wife, "Crazy" George Arnisith and his wife, and most especially a wild, bullshitting marine by the name of Sergio Ortiz.

Throughout the years, while in the service or out, it has been my experience that all marines are full of bullshit. Whether it was Charlie Smith, former state treasurer of Wisconsin; Rick Eilert of Chicago, who published an excellent book on Vietnam; Steve Markley of Kansas; or my dear friend, former governor and congressman Bill Janklow of South Dakota; they all had two things in common: they were all marines and they were incredible bullshitters. Ortiz, however, was in a league of his own. Years later, when my DINFOS friends would get together, Sergio would say something outlandish, and we would all turn to his then-wife Donna, who would either slowly shake her head no or would say, "That's no bullshit." In other words, a second source was mandatory with Sergio.

In spite of this marine bullshit tendency, I loved my "Jar Heads" one and all.

(I used to kid marines about how they would search for land mines. I told them they would put their fingers in their ears, shut their eyes, and walk forward.)

The school itself was excellent. It was not unusual for our instructors to be full bull colonels, and they were good. We were learning to be photographers and reporters for our country's military, and they apparently took that seriously.

Once graduated, we would be assigned to Public Information Offices (PIO) throughout the world, and then would report "all the news that is fit to report" regarding our nation's military.

However, one of the first terms I was taught at DINFOs was "I can neither confirm nor deny," and it quickly dawned on me that "information"—as in U.S. Army public information—bore the same relationship that "intelligence" bore to army intelligence. Oxymorons all.

VIETNAM AND RUMORS OF VIETNAM:

As idyllic as all this was at Uncle Ben's Rest Home, one thing still hung over us like a pall—Vietnam. I had the feeling that the North Vietnamese would not distinguish me from a regular infantry soldier just because I was carrying a Pentax single-lens reflex 35-millimeter camera, notepad, .45 pistol, and a gold Army Correspondent patch over my divisional insignia.

Also, "combat photographer" had a nasty ring, in my opinion.

As our training progressed, however, and our tension mounted as to our fate after the "Rest Home," one of my buddies (Harmon, I think) made a discovery. He had been studying the disposition of previous classes and realized that every other class went to Vietnam while the other class either stayed here in the States or went to Germany.

Sure enough, he was right. With military precision, every other class was deployed in that manner. One to Vietnam, one not, with classes graduating on a regular basis. We quickly counted ahead and with great joy and celebration realized we were on the non-Vietnam count.

We had it made—me in particular, because I was just a two-year draftee. If they didn't send me to Nam right out of DINFOS, I would not even have one year left to complete a tour.

I could see it now—me taking pictures of camp commanders and their fat wives cutting ribbons at the new PX at Fort Hood, Texas. Better yet, Stuttgart, Germany, with the weekends free to explore my ancestral roots, as both sides of my family are of German descent.

(In fact, I know some in my family always wondered about some of our lineage still in the Old Country, and how they might have spent World War II. One perverse older cousin used to tell a story about how we had a relative who had died in a Nazi concentration camp, and when someone would ask him how, he would say, "He fell from a guard tower at Dachau.")

I immediately went out and bought a book entitled *101 Useful German Phrases*. Another bullet dodged—in this case, perhaps quite literally.

While all of this was going on, in our nation's capital the wheels of White House Communications were grinding ever so slowly in my direction.

Quite frankly, I had forgotten all about this possibility once I had not been forced into 11 Bravo; but they, it seems, had not forgotten about me. So on a cold January day, I was summoned and told two Secret Service agents were here to interview me.

If you went to central casting in Hollywood, you could not have found two guys who better fit the description of "government spooks." Both humorless, almost comically serious types, who spoke in that monotonous, cryptic way of all good spies and undercover agents. They plausibly might have uttered the phrase: "If I tell you that, I will have to kill you." They looked as if they were cookie-cut out of the same mold, and I swear if one of them had smiled, both of their faces would have cracked.

They told me that they would now interview me for White House Communications, and so began this weird, almost surreal questioning, whereby they would take turns rapid-firing questions at me. Below is a sampling of their questions, followed by my thoughts (not answers):

"Have you ever done drugs?" (No, but I'm looking forward to the experience.)

"Have you ever knowingly had sex with a communist?" (Yes, there was a whole house full of loose communist girls just down the street from my home in Mitchell, South Dakota.)

"Have you ever had sex with an animal?" (Whoa, there, cowboy, I come from South Dakota, not North Dakota.)

Anyway, Spook 1 and Spook 2 kept this up for what seemed like an hour. When they were finally satisfied that I was not a drug-addicted, commie-screwing, sheep-loving pervert, we finally got down to the details of the job. As mentioned before, I would be located in one of three places: the White House, Key Biscayne, or San Clemente—not shabby duty stations.

Again, because of my love for government and politics, I was convinced this could have been a great way to serve in the army, and I was about to say yes when either Tweedledee or Tweedledum mentioned one last thing: "Ah, you see Private First Class Volk, there's a catch." Because of all the training they were going to have to give me to route Nixon's phone calls, I would have to sign up for an additional year.

Another year! So then what happens? Someday H.R. "Bob" Haldeman doesn't like how I answer the phone, and I am on my way to becoming a gate guard on the DMZ in Vietnam.

I am sure if I and my genius classmates hadn't unlocked the secrets of the rotation of classes that showed us we were surely not going to Vietnam, I would have taken the White House job and taken my chances with old "Bob." But now? I was on my to Germany or some cushy stateside job; no way was I signing up for another year.

President Richard Milhous Nixon was going to have to communicate without PFC David Volk.

One might ask at this point why I had given up probably one of the best MOS's in the army only to end up in Vietnam. Obviously, something went very wrong.

As my colleagues and I approached the end of our DINFOS training, still confident that our next assignments were not going to be in Vietnam, Susan and I started wondering if I could have leave after Fort Ben. So one day I went over to S-1 (personnel) and asked a wizened old civilian lady with a cigarette dangling out of her mouth (remember, this is 1970) if I would qualify for leave after DINFOS. She asked me where my next post was, and I told her I didn't know. So this ancient crone went over to a huge book—much like I am sure Saint Peter has at the Pearly Gates—and out of the side her mouth (as she had not once removed her cigarette) she asked, "What's your name?" "Volk," I replied, and she started running her bony finger down the roster.

"Vaughn. Vogt. Voight. Volk, David—You're going to Vietnam."

This couldn't be! We had it all figured out! The rotations were like clockwork!

I asked her to check again, as I was sure she had smoke in her eyes and had misread my name. She said, "I'll check again, but you're still going to Vietnam, Volk."

I guess it was the casualness of her announcement that shocked me the most, as if she were sending me down the street to buy her more smokes.

When I gathered with my classmates, I tried to cheer them up by saying that "just because I was going perhaps they weren't." But they knew that was B.S. The rotations were off, but the different classes were always one hundred percent either "go" or "no go." We were all screwed.

What had gone wrong? What had we missed that had now put us all on the road to Vietnam? How could we have miscalculated?

We rechecked the levies (disposition of the different classes) and, sure enough, we were right: Every other class went to Vietnam, with the other one going to Europe or staying in CONUS (Continental United States).

Then it hit us! The holidays! The holidays, you idiots! You remember the holidays—turkey with dressing, trees with bright lights, Auld Lang Syne. We hadn't factored in the days we would have off for the holidays, and which had obviously thrown off the levies. Since there was a class graduating almost every two weeks, it did not take but a few days off to throw the rotations off.

Now, it would have been one thing if my brilliant cohorts and I had failed to factor in All Saints Day or Bastille Day, but not to see Thanksgiving and Christmas coming and realize that those extra days off might affect where our class would be stationed!

So I sadly put away my book of *101 Useful German Phrases* and quickly learned the words to the popular song of that time: "All we are saying is give peace a chance."

Oh, where were my "spooks" from White House Communications? Come back, please.

CHAPTER 5

PREPARING FOR WAR.

Things got a little hazy as I prepared to go to war. I remember packing Susan's Camaro with our meager belongings and sending her back west to her parents in South Dakota.

I was off to Fort Riley, Kansas, for Vietnam training on the prairie. What a joke! Going through a simulated Vietnamese village in a half a foot of Kansas snow just wouldn't work.

It was a typical army bullshit operation and did nothing to prepare anyone for Vietnam. In fact, the most vivid memory I had took place off base one Saturday.

Kansas back then had to have the weirdest liquor laws on the planet. Drinking involved joining a club, buying a bottle, leaving your driver's license until you left the premises, turning around three times, putting your finger next to your nose, and promising to go to church on Sunday, or some such nonsense.

All this goofiness was probably the result of some unholy marriage between the last remnants of the Temperance League, who wanted to feel they were still fighting demon rum, and shifty, sot politicians who were more than happy to cater to them as long as they could create enough loopholes to keep their fellow Kansans sufficiently oiled after jumping through their stupid hoops.

There was, however, one hoop my fellow GIs could not jump through—age. I was the only one who was over 21.

As they showed us the door, I could not help but ponder the irony of all this. Here were these young men, who in a few short weeks would be flown to the other side of the world, armed with the most sophisticated weapons known to man, and be expected to kill their fellow human beings. However, in Manhattan, Kansas, on a Saturday night, they couldn't buy a beer.

In spite of where we were that evening, the words from the "The Wizard of Oz" once more came back to me: "I have a feeling we're not in Kansas anymore, Toto."

OAKLAND/SAN FRANCISCO:

We did have leave before going to Vietnam, and Suderman, "Crazy" George, Ortiz, Harmon, and I—along with our wives—spent a wonderful few days in San Francisco before reporting to Oakland—and deployment.

As our days wound down to a precious few, Keith Harmon announced that there was a twenty-four-hour grace period coming off leave, so we could have an extra day. Sounded good to us. As is often the case in the army: "Ah, there is a catch, PFC Harmon." Yes, there was a twenty-four-hour "grace" period after leave; however, it did not apply when reporting for overseas duty. So in addition to everything else, we all got Article 15s upon reporting to Oakland.

Now that I think about it, Harmon was also the one who came up with the sure fire, no Vietnam rotation theory back at Fort Ben. Although he was a good friend, I was really hoping that Harmon would not be stationed with me in Vietnam. So far, his advice and direction had gotten me to blow off White House Communications only to get sent to Vietnam, and now he had me getting fined and punished by the army with an Article 15. I was quite sure if we were together in Vietnam, he would get me killed stone dead.

(As it turned out, we were not stationed by each other in Vietnam—although not as I would have preferred. Harmon ended up being billeted in a hotel in Saigon a block from one of the niftiest whorehouses in Southeast Asia. I, on the other hand, ended up hell and gone up north in Hard Core, I Corp, where on a clear day in a helicopter I could see both the DMZ and the "Valley of Death," the dreaded A Shau. The lucky bastard.)

BUILDING 24:

The most memorable thing about the Oakland processing center for Vietnam was an almost total lack of discipline. Some poor sergeant would come into our billeting area and tell us to hold it down or go to bed, and a dozen guys would yell, "Fuck you! What are you going to do, send us to Vietnam?"

Another interesting aspect of this billeting area was, strangely enough, the latrines. Written on the stall walls were some of the most poignant and heart-moving messages I have ever read. All penned by guys headed off to war. I wish I had copied some of it down, as it was truly inspired graffiti.

To this heartfelt collection, I added a poem from my favorite poet, A.E. Houseman:

> The street sounds to the soldiers' tread,
> And out we troop to see:
> A single redcoat turns his head,
> He turns and looks at me.
>
> My man, from sky to skys so far,
> We never crossed before;
> Such league apart the world's ends are,
> We're like to meet no more;
>
> What thoughts at heart have you and I,
> We cannot stop to tell;
> But dead or living, drunk or dry,
> Soldier, I wish you well.

Every morning at Oakland, hundreds of us would form up in a sloppy formation, and names were called to fall out. After about one hundred names were called, those soldiers were marched off to a place called Building 24, which was your last stop before leaving for Vietnam.

When my name was finally called, the thing I remember most vividly was, when I started marching off to Building 24, there were some crows on a telephone wire, and their caws had a derisive, mocking quality. I remember it shook me some.

Building 24 was a huge warehouse affair with bunk beds that were four or five high. The latrine was a long gutter affair for pissing and approximately fifty commodes running down the wall with no partitions between them. Damn, I wish I had taken a picture as it was truly a sight.

I cannot remember how long we were at Building 24, but not long. In the middle of the night we were woken up and headed to the airport and Vietnam.

CHAPTER 6

"AND IT'S ONE, TWO, THREE, WHAT ARE WE FIGHTING FOR, WELL I DON'T GIVE A DAMN, NEXT STOP IS VIETNAM."

There is only one word that describes a plane trip from Oakland, California, to the Republic of Vietnam: long.

We were on some huge plane from some private contractor called Flying Tiger airlines, and not only was the flight long and tedious, but about halfway there, two hundred GIs crammed together into a small space with everyone smoking, the lot of us giving off an aroma that is difficult to describe.

Our first stop was Hawaii, where I waited hopefully for the basic training rumor to be fulfilled, whereby I would be miraculously pulled from the plane and then spend the rest of my tour as a lifeguard on Waikiki Beach tending to the swimming needs of nurses. Not bloody likely.

Our next stop: Guam or Wake Island. This was starting to get real.

I think two of the most fearful times I had in Vietnam were landing at Bien Hoa airport near Saigon, and taking off to come home eleven months later from Cam Rahn Bay.

The landing was terrifying because it was night and our plane was totally dark. As we looked down, all we could see were red tracers being fired. It looked like we were landing on Omaha Beach on June 6, 1944.

Of course, what we didn't know was that red tracers always denoted American fire, since the NVA used either green or no tracers. What we were probably seeing was a "mad-minute," whereby everyone along a perimeter opens fire, both to check their weapons and to hopefully catch an enemy sapper in the wire. However, to a bunch of FNGs (Fucking New Guys) in a darkened plane, it looked like the end of the world.

Eleven months later, when I was again on a plane waiting to take off, I think my dread was even worse. I had made it! All that was left was for this plane to take off and go back to "The World."

We seemed to sit on the tarmac for a very long time, and I just knew a stray mortar round or 155 rocket was going to find us just as we were ready to come home. Finally, as we took off, two hundred soldiers willed our "Freedom Bird" off the runway, and then we made that beautiful bank out over the South China Sea. Damn few things in my life have been as exhilarating.

CLUSTER FUCK PERSONIFIED:

There are two things you notice in getting off a plane in Vietnam: one is the incredible humidity, and the second is the smell. The smell wasn't necessarily unpleasant—just very different.

Then I saw some Vietnamese, with their conical hats and long gowns, being processed through a gate. It finally registered that, not only wasn't I in Kansas anymore, I was one hell of a long way from Kansas.

We were all numb with fatigue, so processing in was all a blur. The only thing that vividly sticks out is when about two hundred of us were in a small Quonset hut, seated on folding chairs and getting a lecture on venereal disease.

We were told that there was a hybrid strain of VD over here that did not respond to any known cure. If you were unlucky enough to get this disease, called the "Black Syph," you would be sent to an island and would spend the rest of your short life watching body parts fall off.

Anyway, at some point during this totally worthless lecture, we heard a "whump." Now, we had been hearing loud bangs since arriving and were reassured it was "outgoing"—which was good.

However, this had a different sound, and when another, closer "whump" sounded, we all started to nervously look around. The third and loudest "whump" came, and someone yelled "Incoming!" This was not good. Anyway, two hundred "cherries" headed for a small door. (A "cherry" was a new guy who hadn't seen combat yet, and so still possessed some sort of a lack-of-combat hymen. The term "cluster fuck" was given new meaning that day.)

Now, one of my DINFOS buddies who had accompanied me to Vietnam was Weird George, a rather small guy with thick glasses. Anyway, as I headed to the door with the other two hundred idiots, I looked back to see George tangled in a mountain of discarded folding chairs, and since it didn't look like I was going anywhere fast, I went back and untangled him, and we headed for the door and a bunker. (We laughed about this years later, but it was not funny at the time.)

Now, if the goofy army would have taught us what to do during a rocket attack rather than some bullshit about a mythical disease called the "Black Syph," we would have been better off, since the last thing you ever do during a rocket attack is get up and run. You hit the deck and try and get to something that will give you some protection.

I swear if the VC, who had fired those 155mm rockets, had brought one more there would have been a shit-pot full of dead and wounded cherries.

Weird George and I finally found a bunker. Next to me was an E-7 lifer with hash marks up his sleeve. (One hash mark denoted three years in the army.) Anyway, this E-7 said, "What the hell am I doing here?" I looked at him in shock. "What the hell are you doing here?!" I thought. "You're a career soldier; what the hell am I doing here? I'm a teacher!"

I had two other thoughts while sitting in that bunker waiting for the all-clear siren to blow. My first was: "I am in country only a few hours, and someone has already tried to kill me. No way in hell am I making 364 days and a wake-up."

The second thought—equally disturbing—involved the very notion that someone wanted to kill me. As I have mentioned, I grew up in a quiet Midwest town that probably had a murder every ten years, whether we needed one or not.

The biggest danger I remember growing up was getting the shit beat out of me by Terry Hohn, a seventeen-year-old eighth-grader. Not that I probably didn't have it coming, as I had a smart mouth back in those days. However, the idea that someone I did not know, and had never done any harm to, wanted to kill me, was a very disturbing proposition.

SCREAMING EAGLES:

Things did not get much better after the rocket attack, as my buddy Dan Suderman and I were informed that we would be assigned to the 101st Airborne Division, Screaming Eagles, which was stationed in the very northern part of the country.

As we were standing behind the stake that indicated what division we were going to, an NCO came by and said, "Damn, you're going up north to 'Hard Core, I Corp' with the Screaming Eagles? Fucking gooks come screaming out of the jungles in the middle of day, lobbing mortars on your head up there."

While I sensed that fucking with cherries was probably high sport there at Long Binh, I also felt that making "364 and a wake-up" was still fading fast.

We flew a C-130 up to our division. A C-130 is not so much an airplane as a flying boiler room. At least that was what the interior looked and sounded like to me.

Processing into the 101st was fairly routine, except for a couple of incidents I remember.

We were walking down a line of typists who were very boringly getting us enrolled into the unit. In fact, there was a huge sign that read: "Life is Just a Bowl of Cherries." As I gave my papers to one guy he said, "You're from South Dakota? So am I—Rapid City." So we started the usual "Do you know so and so."

This conversation was going pretty well until I told him that I went to Northern State College, and he said his girlfriend went to Northern. I asked who she was, and he said: "Mary Ellwein." Now, I had dated a Mary Ellwein from Rapid City for almost two years while we were in college, so I somewhat delicately asked him when he had dated her and, sure enough, it was during the same time. I never told him about our overlapping love of Mary Ellwein, as pissing off "clerk jerks" was bad karma. The next thing you know, your paycheck is going to Boise, Idaho, and your mail to Seoul, South Korea.

It did seem somewhat strange that I had to come to the other side of the planet to find out that my darling Mary had two-timed me.

Another incident involved ignoring a time-honored maxim of army life and was probably a good lesson to learn early in my stay in Vietnam. The maxim was: "Never volunteer for anything."

Once processed through division, there were about thirty of us in a formation, and one of the clerks came out and asked if anyone could type. Now, upon arriving at Camp Evans, where SERTS (Screaming Eagle Replacement Training Station) was located, I had seen some guys doing some nasty jobs. Filling sand bags, digging bunkers by hand, doing police calls, and so forth.

So I figured typing had to be better than any of those jobs, and a few fellow typists and I stepped forward. The clerk jerk then said, "Alright, the rest of you guys are free to go." So while my buddies spent the afternoon at the EM Club drinking beer, I spent it typing in a building that had to be 120 degrees. I never volunteered again.

Finally, I remember at SERTS my buddy Suderman and me going to a USO show. One of the songs the band sang was by The Animals, and they had changed the lyrics to: "We got to get out of this place, if it's the last thing we ever do, we got to get out of this place...there's a better life in the USA." We got to laughing, for here we were just six days in country, singing our hearts out like we were hardened veterans.

Also that evening we were sitting with a Vietnamese interpreter and a Chieu Hoi—an NVA soldier who had come over to our side and become a Kit Carson scout. We bought them beer, joked, laughed, sang songs, and had a grand time. Later it brought to mind a poem by Thomas Hardy called "The Man He Killed" and was about killing someone who, if you had met under different circumstances, would have probably become friends with. The last stanza of that poem was:

"Yes; quaint and curious war is!
You shoot a fellow down
You'd treat, if met where any bar is,
Or help to half a crown."

Anyway, I found the whole thing strangely disquieting, as this former North Vietnamese soldier did not appear like someone I wanted to kill regardless of the circumstances.

After our SERTS training, which like the Fort Riley, Kansas, training was totally tits-on-a-boar worthless, both Suderman and I were assigned to Camp Eagle, home of the first brigade and divisional headquarters. I hated it.

Although there was not much danger of getting sent to the bush and into harm's way, as we handled not only the publication of our weekly newspaper *The Screaming Eagle*, but also our monthly magazine *Rendezvous With Destiny* and finally our division's yearbook. Yes, just like high school we had a yearbook. (I always imagined at the end of our year in Vietnam of going around and signing each other's yearbook: "Hey, Lefty, sorry about that booby trap thing.")

Now, with all of this to do at division headquarters, your chances of remaining a REMF (Rear-Echelon Motherfucker) were pretty good, as most of the actual stories from the field were handled by the Brigade Public Information Offices (PIOs). However, division was a hellhole, where you couldn't swing a dead cat without hitting some harassing senior NCO or officer with nothing better to do than screw with you because your moustache was too long, your boots were not shined, you hadn't saluted, etc. Add to that it was also incredibly boring.

I pleaded with a second lieutenant friend of mine, Pinnell, to get me transferred to 3rd Brigade up north of Hue at Camp Evans. Even though my chances of having to go to the field and actually get into combat would greatly increase up there, I would do anything to get out of Camp Eagle and its bullshit.

As I think back, it seems very strange, and quite frankly it greatly increased my chances of getting killed. At the time it seemed the perfect thing to do.

Lieutenant Pinnell and I had become friends because he loved to gamble, and among the lower officers one of their favorite gambling activities was betting on foosball at the Officers Club. Because of my misspent youth at college, I was an excellent foosball player, so every once in a while Pinnell would pin a set of his 2nd Louie "butter bars" on me, and off we would go to the officer's club to clean up.

Pinnell finally agreed to get me transferred to 3rd Brigade. "Ah, but Spec. 4 Volk, there is a catch." The catch was that before I could go to 3rd Brigade I had to do a magazine article complete with pictures on the LRPs (Long Range Patrol), the Airborne Rangers.

Suddenly that marching cadence from basic came back: "I want to be an Airborne Ranger, I want to live a life of danger."

Incredibly, I agreed, so strong was my desire to get away from the hassles and boredom at divisional headquarters. As I said, today it makes no sense.

The Airborne Rangers were an elite group who operated in five- or six-man teams and were inserted far from our bases to try and determine enemy troop movements coming down the Ho Chi Minh Trail.

Sometimes they were even in Laos and Cambodia (being "over the fence," as we called it), although no one would admit to that either then or now. My time with them was very rewarding, and quite frankly when we did go to the bush I felt safer than I would later when I would be surrounded by a whole company of infantrymen. The rangers had their "shit grouped," as we said, and did not make mistakes.

My magazine article and pictures (some of which ran in the States) were probably some of my best work.

However, this whole series of events involving my transfer to 3rd Brigade had a certain weird feel to it, and I was becoming aware that weird was becoming the norm.

CHAPTER 7

"GOOD MORNING, VIETNAM" Daily Life in the RVN.

As mentioned at the beginning of this tale, I think that too much of the details of history are lost. What was it like to be an ordinary soldier, day to day, in the RVN? I will try and explain.

Housing. Like everything else in Vietnam, how you were housed depended on where you were. As I already noted, that lucky bastard Keith Harmon was in a hotel in Saigon right in the middle of whorehouse heaven.

In the 101st, if you lived in a base camp (Phu Bai—2nd Brigade; Eagle—headquarters and 1st Brigade; Evans—3rd Brigade) you lived in a hooch, a wooden affair that had plywood running up two-thirds of the walls and then finished with a screen with shutters and a tin roof. The whole hooch was placed about two feet off the ground.

With any luck, there were only four or five guys in the hooch, because then you could use the back third of the hooch and put in a bar, refrigerator, dart board, etc. Sand bags generally ran up halfway around the shack, and at Camp Evans, which was a little more remote and vulnerable than the other base camps, there were underground bunkers that generally served five or six hooches. Each soldier had a somewhat partitioned off area in the hooch. These hooches were also home to countless mice that you could hear scurrying about all night, interrupted every so often by the sound of a trap snapping shut to kill one of the little bastards.

Food: There was definitely a food chain when it came to eating where I was stationed. The worst food came out of the army mess. I swear to God the army planned the same menus for U.S. soldiers everywhere in the world and would not stray from it.

On a day when it was 110 degrees in the shade, these idiots would serve boiled roast beef, lumpy potatoes, and gravy. Regardless of what they served, it was almost always bad.

Moving up the food chain, the second best thing to eat, believe it or not, was C-Rations (C-Rats). Supposedly surplus from World War II, they came in little tins and were opened with a thing called a P-38, which was a small can opener device you carried around your neck with your dog tags.

Quite frankly, if you could heat C-Rats, they weren't too bad. However, without heat there was a gelatinous substance on the top that looked like the stuff that Bill Murray gets slimed with in "Ghostbusters."

If C-Rats had any problem, it was that they had no taste, which is why dehydrated onions and bottles of Tabasco sauce were cherished possessions.

In fact, one of the most poignant moments I would experience in Vietnam came while eating C-Rats. I was on a brand new firebase called Barnett, way out in the boonies. We lived underground in bunkers, and this was during the monsoon. In short order our bunkers resembled the trenches of World War I. Mud, ankle deep.

We bought cheap Vietnamese hammocks to sleep in and used empty ammo crates to keep everything else out of the water and muck.

One night we had taken the back off a claymore mine (a nasty weapon, which was a little smaller, then the size of today's laptop computers. It had C-4 explosive in the back, which when detonated by a handheld device called a clacker propelled ball bearings in a 60-degree fan-shaped pattern.) However, when the C-4 was removed and used in small amounts, it could be used to heat food. Anyway, about four of us were sitting around in this depressing, muddy hellhole; it was Saturday night and we were getting ready to eat.

Finally, one of the guys took out the last of his dehydrated onions and poured it into his dirty hand. He then proceeded to go around to each of us and measure out a little into our C-Rations.

Because of some of the positions I have held throughout my life and travels, I have dined in some of the best restaurants in this country, including the White House. Also, because I have always been blessed with the wonderful friends I have, almost always dined in good company. However, I must say that few dinners have meant as much as that one on muddy Firebase Barnett, when a generous fellow GI squeezed some flaked onions from his dirty hand into my chicken and noodles.

The fruit in C-Rats were prized; however, one stayed away from the peanut butter. Not only did it have the consistency of industrial strength glue, but it could also stop you up for weeks. There was a hot chocolate package that was good when you could get it heated, especially during the monsoon season.

I always liked chicken and noodles and tried to avoid "beans and dicks" (hot dogs and beans) and "beans and motherfuckers" (lima beans and ham). The crackers tasted as if they were surplus hard tack from the Civil War. Of course, there was also a nice little packet of four cigarettes in each C-Rats box. Ah, thank you, Mr. Philip Morris.

At the pinnacle of the food pyramid was the crème de la crème of eating, the four-star food of Vietnam: the Long Range Patrol Packets (LRPs). Dehydrated food in a heavy plastic bag, which when mixed with water was damn fine dining.

I swear to God, to this day I get a craving for a beef hash LRP; however, all of them were delicious.

Unfortunately, like so many things in Vietnam, the guys who deserved them most—the grunts at the front—almost never got them. There were a number of reasons for this.

First and probably foremost is that the REMFs got first crack at them. Also, especially during the summer, when you had to hump a lot of water, LRPs took a lot of water. And it was rumored that grunts who had seen enough of the war would sometimes eat the LRPs without water, and of course the dehydrated mixer would quickly soak up their stomach fluids and they would have to be medivaced to the rear.

   Once when I was inserted to a line unit, I took one LRP with me, and while the grunts ate their cold C-Rats I had the LRP. I never felt more like an asshole in my life, and I never did it again.

   We seldom ate Vietnamese food. Their main dish seemed to be rice covered by a sauce called *nuoc-mam*, which was created by putting dead fish in a can and placing it in the ground or out in the sun until it fermented into a foul-smelling sauce. There was a French bread we would sometimes buy from vendors in Hue, which was delicious and had an aroma that came right from bread heaven.

   WEAPONS—EQUIPMENT:

   The M16 was the standard weapon for us in Vietnam and, quite frankly, I always felt that it was ill-suited for fighting in a triple canopy jungle. Its high velocity 5.56mm bullet just did not seem effective in heavy cover.

   Depending on where I was going and how dangerous I thought it would be, I would often carry just a .45 pistol—an incredibly inaccurate weapon, and which in my hands posed no danger to the enemy unless he was standing right in front of me. Otherwise, I carried an M16 with a long strap so the weapon hung down in front me and I could still use my camera.

   Even more worthless in the jungle was the M60 grenade launcher, a nasty-looking weapon, but not very practical in heavy foliage. I always figured the chances were about 50-50 that the damn grenade, when fired, would hit something and drop on us.

   The same could be said for the LAAW, a shoulder-fired 66mm rocket made of fiberglass and disposable after one shot.

By far the best weapon an infantry company possessed was the M60 machine gun. This damn thing put bullets (7.62mm) where you were looking and almost always accounted for kills in the bush. Everyone always carried additional ammo for this gun.

Because we mostly operated in the jungle, we had to carry huge rucksacks, generally with four or five days' worth of rations and ammunition. Add to that entrenching tools, water, etc., these could run to fifty pounds or more.

I remember one time when some guys from the Big Red One Division ("If you gotta be one, be a Red One") were transferred to us when their colors went home. (Division was sent home but their time wasn't up yet.)

Anyway, these guys from the 1st Division were standing on a firebase as we got off our choppers. Now they had been operating down in the delta and had never carried anything heavier than a "day pack." As we peeled off these huge rucks, the Red One guys stared in shock. Finally one of them said, "Damn, where do you put the wheels on that motherfucker?"

MISCELLANEOUS:
Life in the rear was mostly work, boredom, and drinking. One day was absolutely like the next, and Sunday was no different than Wednesday.

Your evenings were spent at the Enlisted Men's Club. However, I did make a point to observe a time-honored tradition from my part of the country and always showered and put on clean fatigues for Saturday night.

Not that it was any different than any other night, or that there would be anything resembling a woman there, but it just seemed like the thing to do.

From those of us who drank there was a separate group of people who did drugs, mostly marijuana. I never handled that very well, and the few times I tried it became either violently ill or incredibly paranoid.

Also, in the rear there was an ugly undercurrent of racial tension. Blacks—who had long rituals of handshakes, arm-slapping greetings, and power salutes—often segregated themselves, and there were some redneck groups that had their own clubs and sat together in mess halls. All luxuries of being a REMF. I never saw any of that shit in the bush.

AFVN radio was very good, and even long after he had departed we were awakened with Adrian Cronauer's "GOOD MORNING, VIETNAM!" We had a black-and-white TV, but the reception and choice of channels was right out of the fifties. We could buy stereo equipment and other merchandise out of a catalog from something called PACEX, which was a type of mail-order post exchange. It was cheap and high quality, and no hooch worth its salt did not have a hell of a sound system.

We took a leak in a thing called a "piss tube," which was a fifty-gallon drum cut in half and planted in the ground on top of rocks. Shitting was done in good old-fashioned outhouses — again into fifty-gallon drums cut in half. When they got full they were picked up and taken out and burned with gasoline.

Our showers were again plywood shacks with screens two-thirds up. A huge water tank sat on top, and they operated much like you see in the old "MASH" TV shows. The water was not heated (at least not for enlisted men), which was fine in the summer. However, during the monsoon season, when everything you owned got wet and clammy, a cold shower was horrible. I swore I would never take hot showers for granted again, but I obviously have.

Even something like guard duty on a big base camp like Evans was more hassle and boredom than actual danger. There were large cement bunkers that surrounded the camp with all kinds of concertina wire, claymores, foo gas canisters, etc. Damn near impregnable.

There were four of us to a bunker, and two would be on guard duty and two would sleep. We had a small tent with two cots in it, and we were even brought food during the night. Not exactly hard duty.

We would never even think of actually going into the bunkers, since they were controlled by large, ugly rats. I mean nasty, small-dog-sized rats. We pretty much struck a deal with them that if we would leave them alone and share our food with them they would leave us alone.

They truly were some big rats. We used to see them running to other bunkers—I'm sure for some wild rat bunker bash. We were warned never to kill them, for they carried nasty vermin that went looking for somewhere else to live if the body went cold. I was always reluctant to take a shot at them anyway. I was such a poor marksman I figured I would just wound one of them enough to piss 'im off and he would turn and attack me.

I suppose they got so big because many years before their ancestors decided to join our side and live well on American garbage. I'm sure their country cousins, who traveled with the NVA, were of a much leaner variety.

Again, all of the above amenities were luxuries enjoyed by those in base camps or firebases. Life in the field was not nearly so comfortable.

EVERYONE IS EQUAL; HOWEVER, SOME ARE MORE EQUAL THAN OTHERS:
I don't know how things were in other wars as it pertained to how REMFs and soldiers on the line lived. However, I cannot believe there has ever been a war where the lines between the two were more dramatically marked than in Vietnam.

There truly were the "haves" (those in the rear) and the "have-nots" (those in the field), and to someone like myself, who traveled a great deal between the two, the contrast was very stark indeed.

By 1970, if you were stationed in one of the large base camps or large firebases, you lived a pretty good life. Three hots and a cot, nice living quarters, TV, plenty to drink and smoke, and most importantly, relative safety.

We totally controlled the lowlands up north by that time, and I safely hitchhiked up Highway 1 throughout my tour. Outside of an isolated rocket attack, once in a while you would have been hard pressed to even know there was a war going on. (By the way, if you were killed in a 155mm rocket attack your number was just up, for this was a weapon the enemy leaned up against a bamboo pole and fired like 4th of July rockets. Absolutely random shots fired into a huge area.)

Being out in the shit was a totally different experience. Miserable conditions, miserable food, no booze, mind-numbing physical exertion, fatigue, and just to top it all off, a good chance of getting into combat and really having something bad happen. I need to add something about fatigue, because it deserves more than just a passing comment. On any given night in the field, you were lucky to get a few hours of restless sleep, and it seemed less than that during the monsoon. Bugs were everywhere in Vietnam, and during the cold, wet monsoon season they did what all creatures do in that situation—they looked for someplace warm and dry to crawl into. Since I grew up in the Midwest, I was no stranger to bugs. (In neighboring Minnesota, the mosquito is the state bird.) Nothing, though, could have prepared me for the swirling swarms of pests in Vietnam. We used to say that you could tell how long people had been "in country" by how they handled bugs in their drinks. If they were "cherry", they threw the entire drink away. If they had been around for a while, they used their fingers to fish the bugs out. If they had been in Nam for a long time, they just drank the drink, bugs and all.

Anyway, after a sleepless night you then could be on the move all day in jungle-like mountainous terrain with a heavy pack. Even if you did not make contact, soldiers in the field for a long length of time would have that blankness in their eyes of the "thousand-yard stare," and young boys would look many years older.

As I said, perhaps these kinds of dichotomy and contrasts have always existed between people at the front and rear lines; however, I am sure the total lack of senior NCOs and officers anywhere near the front lines had to be unique to Vietnam—at least up north, where I was stationed.

I moved about the entire 101st Airborne Division and did time in all three brigades, and I never saw any officer above the rank of captain, or an NCO above the rank of staff sergeant in the bush. Now perhaps that was not the case in other areas of Vietnam, where large unit operations were more prevalent, as we almost exclusively traveled in company-size units, which were commanded by a captain. However, there just seemed to be such a gulf between those in the rear and those in the field, and I always thought there would have been a lot less chickenshit army hassling going on if more officers and senior NCOs actually got out of their air-conditioned bunkers and went to the front once in a while. Most battalion commanders operated from what was called a "C & C" (combat and control) helicopter, and remained well above any battles.

In addition to my combat photography and news reporting duties, I also escorted civilian correspondents into the field. I got to know some of the big names in network news during this time (Steve Bell, Frank Mariano, and others).

I remember one night drinking with some civilian photographers, and I asked this one guy how long he had been in country. He said, "Since Dien Bien Phu." It was Henri Huet, the Pulitzer Prize-winning photographer who took the incredible photograph of the wounded GI reaching up for help and cradling the head of his dying buddy during the battle of Dak To.

Huet was featured in the book *Lost Over Laos*, which my buddy Ortiz did most of the photo work for.

When it came to escorting correspondents to the field, I always wanted network types, as they had a certain degree of self-preservation in their outlook. The worst were the freelance photographers, who were always looking for action.

They only got paid if they photographed something really graphic—combat stuff—so their first question, when coming into our office and looking at our AO (area of operation) map, was: "Who's making contact"?

Lying to these bastards became an art form. I told this one hot dog that this unit here in the lowlands was making a lot of contact. When we got to the unit, a bunch of grunts were sitting around an old, burned-out French railroad depot, smoking and joking; all the while little Vietnamese kids were coming out from a nearby village, selling us cold Cokes. This freelancer looks at me and says, "This unit is making a lot of contact?"

To which I replied, "Damn, things must have quieted down for them."

I hated freelancers. They would come breezing into our division and want to drag my ass into harm's way for a few days and then catch the next chopper back to Saigon, where they would sit around the Caravel Hotel drinking and swapping war stories with the rest of their sorry bunch.

Fuck 'em; and who knows where danger lurks — one of those Screaming Eagles, there in the lowlands, could have gotten a bad can of Coke, or stumbled on the railroad tracks, or cut himself with a P-38. If you freelance bastards want to see combat, go to the 4th fucking Division in the Central Highlands.

MONEY:

Like everything else, money in Vietnam was strange and, like food, some was better than others.

At the bottom of the money chain was the P, which was the Vietnamese piaster. Damn near worthless, as far as I could ever discern, and not even the Vietnamese wanted to deal with it.

Then there was MPC (Military Payment Currency), which is what we were paid in and used most of the time. It was all paper money, somewhat larger than Monopoly money, with a real paper money feel and all differently colored (the dime might be blue, the dollar orange, the quarter red, etc.).

At least a couple of times while I was in Vietnam the military would slam shut all the bases, and no one could get in or out of them, and you went in and exchanged your MPC for new money. This time the dime might be orange, the dollar red, and so on. All the previous currency of the previous color was worthless, and just so much Monopoly money. Millions and millions had to be lost by black marketers who could not get their money exchanged.

Also, to discourage profiteering, you could only send so much money home each month, and a great guy, Sergeant Garza, who ran the Senior NCO Club and the Enlisted Men's Club, used to have me send money to his family in southern Texas each month, as he was one hell of a poker player. Always wondered what the boys in the post office thought when a guy from Dakota named Volk sent money to a family in Texas named Garza. I will cover him more when I get to the characters chapter of Vietnam.

Obviously, at the top of this economic pyramid was the almighty American dollar, which we were expressly forbidden to have, but did in small quantities. I cannot even remember what the exchange rate of the P was to the MPC, but it seems to me that the MPC to a real American dollar was about 20 to 1. So if you had a $20 bill you had $400 MPCs.

Quite frankly, money did not matter much, because there was nothing to spend it on, and I, in addition to sending some of Garza's surplus gambling money home, also sent money home every month. The only time that did not hold true was the few times I got to Saigon.

Basic Training, Ft. Lewis Washington— —I am in the middle of the first row. Because of my advanced age (22) and advanced education (college grad), I was known as
'Professor'. What a sad sack looking bunch.

My buddies and I in our Tiger fatigues. I'm the one that looks like a bookkeeper for Pancho Villa. Picture was taken just after our adventures in a ville by Eagle Beach.

Military Payment Currency (MPC). This was the money we used in Vietnam. A couple of times during my stay in Vietnam our bases would be closed and you would exchange your MPC for a currency of a different color. Millions had to be lost by black marketers who could not get their money exchanged.

Phu Bai

"I know when I die, I'm going to heaven because I have spent my time in Hell, Phu Bai, Vietnam. Phu Bai was home to the 2nd Brigade of the 101st Airborne Division. Behind the hills in the background are mountatins, jungles and all kind of scary stuff.

"ABANDON ALL HOPE YE WhO ENTER HERE"
DANTE.

Valley of Death —- The A Shau ——Americans tried unsuccessfully to establish bases in the A Shau throughout the war. It was a main artery of he Ho Chi Minh Trail.

Me with an NVA pith helmet that I got while operating with the Cav. It was filled with holes caused by a fle'chette rocket, which shot steel darts, usually to clear foliage. God, was I ever that young and skinny?

No Place for a Picnic

Stark terrain greets these troopers of the 101st Airborne Div. as they move into a clearing to secure a landing zone during operations about 15 miles west of Hue. (USA)

I shot this picture and it illustrates what de-foliants like Agent Orange could do to trees. I just finished my last chemo treatment for follicular lymphoma cancer so trees weren't the only things it affected. We found an NVA cave and cache of weapons shortly after this picture was taken.

2/327 at Tomahawk

Attack foiled

CAMP HOCHMUTH — Quick reactions by the 2nd Bn. (Ambl.), 327th Inf. thwarted enemy attacks on a U.S. installation southeast of Hue recently resulting in 21 enemy killed and three detained.

A four-hour battle at FSB Tomahawk, 25 miles southeast of Hue, began about 1:40 a.m. when an unidentified number of 82mm mortar rounds impacted on the base. A ground attack by enemy sappers accompanied the mortar barrage.

One mortarman with Co. E, Spec. 4 Thomas Jackson, Memphis, Tenn., described his response to the enemy mortars. "It took us only a few seconds to man the tubes and fire illumination. We stayed on until about daybreak before we could take a breather."

"We had been hearing noises all night," explained Sgt. James Skinner of Flint, Mich. "It was then that one of the enemy soldiers tripped a flare and we saw two of them run."

Capt. Robert E. Cox, Decatur, Ill., described the enemy soldiers as being "obviously well-trained." "After the attack," he said, "we found marker stakes they had placed prior to the attack that pointed toward our bunkers, so when they came up in the night they could aim their RPGs. Also, their equipment was well maintained and complete."

A post-battle sweep of the area at dawn by the "No Slack" troopers revealed the 21 NVA dead, eight AK-47 rifles, eight RPG launchers and numerous satchel charges.

This is the story about the attack on Firebase Tomahawk, which I reference in the book. It is typical of reporting I did as an Army Correspondent. All my stories, by the way, were about victories.

The monsoon in Vietnam was miserable. Clouds and rain for days on end. I guess the gloomy, rainy weather at Ft. Lewis was good preparation for this aspect of the war.

SODOM AND GOMORRAH ON THE MEKONG:
I only got to Saigon a couple of times but one trip was truly memorable as I met all of my DINFOs buddies there when we all got weekend passes at the same time.

As I had mentioned, the whole class got shipped over when the rotations got screwed up because of the holidays. Anyway, the whole bunch of us hooked up in Saigon, hosted, of course, by our hotel—by the whorehouse-living, big-city friend Keith Harmon. The rest of us were all stationed in remote areas far from the delights of a place like Saigon.

One of the first things Harmon said to us was, "Now, I don't want you rubes from the boonies coming down here and paying a lot of money for a piece of ass, as it will wreck the whole economy, and the first thing you know those of us who live here will be paying higher prices."

We stood in shocked silence. We had been out in the field for months, with no female companionship, and somehow now we were supposed to be concerned about some delicate economic structure in Saigon whorehouses. What happened next Harmon had coming.

He was right about one thing—we were "rubes." After being away for many weeks from anything close to a city, bars with loose women, and all sorts of other wonderful vices, we hit Saigon like Jethro Bodine and company.

In fact, our lack of urban etiquette almost led to a nasty incident, when Weird George needed to relieve himself and walked down a side street off Tu Do Street and found a jeep wheel. I looked at the back of the jeep and saw the letters ROK. I then looked over and saw some Republic of Korea (ROK) Marines sitting in an outdoor bar, staring at my friend peeing on their jeep wheel. Now, the only thing I had ever heard about ROK Marines was that they were all psychopathic killers. I truly think they were so stunned at the audacity of this strange-looking GI that they were slow to react, and we hustled George away before they could slice us all up into pieces.

There were probably six or seven of us, and I lost track of some of the boys as we hurried from one Sodom-and-Gomorrah bar and honky tonk after the other. I finally saw a friend, Steve Behn, and I asked him where he had been, and he told me he had already been to a whorehouse and had a quickie. "Quickie" probably being the operative word here, since after months without a woman, staying power was not one of our strong suits.

Now at the time, as I remember, you could have the company of a beautiful young lady for the evening for around $30 MPC, so I imagined a quickie cost around $15 MPC.

I asked Behn what he had paid for his quickie, and he got a shit-eating, drunken grin on his face and said, "Twenty dollars American, and an unknown quantity of MPC." I got to laughing so hard I had to sit down on the sidewalk. I would have bet a month's pay that Spec. 4 Steve Behn had just set a new brothel record in Saigon, because based on the local monetary system he had just paid well over $400 MPC for a $15 quickie.

Anyway, I thought it was great and still do. Good for you, Steve Behn, and your incredible generosity to one of Saigon's sporting girls.

I hope every time after that weekend when Harmon walked down to his neighborhood brothel he had to pay more because Steve Behn set a whole new standard. He was probably a legend among the ladies of Tu Do Street for years. "Twenty dollars American and unknown quantity of MPC" indeed!

MISCELLANEOUS SIGHTS AND SOUNDS OF VIETNAM:

Language. Like most wars, the Vietnam War developed a language unique to the conflict, consisting for the most part of a mixture of Vietnamese words and American, a few worded phrases that had a much larger meaning, and the ever-present profanity.

Below are a few examples:

Boo-Coo — bastardized French meaning "a lot."

Boom-boom — sex

Didi mau — go quickly

Dinky dau — crazy

FUBAR — "Fucked Up Beyond All Recognition," a phrase used a lot in Vietnam.

Ghosting — fucking off

Honey dippers — people responsible for burning shit.

Most ricky-tick — immediately, if not sooner.

Number one — best

Number ten — worst

Short — a term used by everyone in Vietnam to tell all who would listen that his tour was almost over. Sometimes quite creatively, as in: "I'm so short I have to rappel out of the bed in the morning." (I should mention here that everyone in Vietnam, from the generals on down to the lowliest privates, had what was called a "short timer's" calendar, which had a voluptuous woman, superimposed on a map of Vietnam. This picture was covered with little squares totaling 365, and you colored in a square each day starting with 365 and working to day one. You can imagine where that day was located on the young lady.)

Tee tee — small

Xin loi — "Sorry about that."

Among people who used radios a lot, there also developed a special language — phrases that only GIs would understand, and a hybrid of army phonetics and slang.

I remember once being inserted, by helicopter, into a line unit, and I overheard the pilot talking to the company commander on the ground. Understand that when a helicopter came to deliver supplies and pick up mail, etc., it never actually landed and everything was unloaded and loaded very quickly.

Helicopters had a nasty way of drawing attention from the enemy, and I always jumped out of them quickly in the field and ran for cover.

Anyway, the chopper pilot had to tell the company commander (CO) that he was inserting someone with the company, and he described me thus: "I have a Clark Kent, puking buzzard type." In other words, he had an army reporter from the 101st Airborne. "Puking Buzzard" was a derogatory description of our divisional patch, the "Screaming Eagle."

Of course, we used derisive terms to describe other divisions and their patches. The 82nd Airborne with its distinctive AAs was called "Almost Airborne." The 1st Cav had a large bright yellow patch with a line that ran diagonally through it and a horse's head in one corner. Of this we would say: "The line that was never crossed, the horse that was never ridden, and the color that explained it all."

After the My Lai massacre, the Americal Division was called "The Americalley Division," in honor of Lieutenant Calley, who supervised the massacre.

Anyone with the MACV patch incurred all kinds of disdain, as that patch was the symbol of pampered, Saigon-residing REMFs.

As I mentioned, there were also short phrases that spoke volumes. One of my favorites was: "It don't mean nothing." It was a stoical comment that we would use when we would have disappointments, such as something bad happening back in the "World'" (U.S.), like a large anti-war protest, a buddy who got a "Dear John" letter, Christmas time, or anything that would sometimes prompt us to be depressed. Invariably, someone would loudly proclaim, "Fuck it. It don't mean nothing."

A way, I guess, of saying: "We're still here, and we still have each other, and we are tougher than tough times."

Once again, I don't feel that I am explaining it very well. It was a soldier thing, and out of context these are sometimes hard to explain.

Christmas time was a particularly depressing time to be away at war, and my heart goes out to our service people who are currently deployed during the holidays. We put up a small, plastic, Charlie Brown type tree, exchanged small gifts, and listened to carols; however, Christmas was a time of year to be endured, not enjoyed, in Vietnam.

Monsoon—As I have noted a couple of times, I grew up on the prairie, in a family of seven that depended on the salary of a used car salesman. (My mother went to work for Penny's when we five boys got older.)

Like most towns in my state, we were heavily dependant on agriculture, and we lived "fat or lean," depending on rain, a situation so precarious that the difference between a good or a bad Christmas might depend on that "Million Dollar" rain that either fell or didn't fall in August.

With that as a background, when I first encountered the monsoons of Vietnam, I thought, "This is good—rain." Then it kept raining and kept raining, and when it wasn't raining it was overcast and drizzly until you finally thought, "Fuck my Midwest upbringing, fuck Million-Dollar Rains, good Christmases, bad Christmases; I just want to see the sun again!"

Soon everything you wore, slept in, stepped in, and ate was damp, clammy, muddy, and cold. In the rear we had "hot boxes" (not what it sounds like), which were small wooden footlockers we put a hundred-watt light bulb in, in an attempt to dry out our socks, especially if you were headed into the field. Jungle rot was as bad as it sounds.

During the day, it would pretty much rain on and off and drizzle constantly; however, usually in the late afternoon, it would not just rain, it would pour.

I remember one time being in the hooch alone when one of these deluges hit. The sound of this downpour hitting a tin roof had a quality that suggested it just could not rain any harder, but it was trying to.

Now this will sound weird, but it reminded me of when you are throwing up, and it just cannot leave your body fast enough.

Toto, how very far I must be from Kansas when I start to think the rain sounds like projectile vomiting.

Anyway, I thought the whole crazy analogy had the potential for a great Bob Dylan song, who could sing, in his nasally way:

"I'm here in Vietnam; there ain't nothing I ain't seen.

I just wish Vietnam would stop its puking on me."

Seriously, I did not use heavy drugs in Vietnam.

The Yellow Brick Road that was going to take me home was getting weirder, and as all of us fans of Gonzo Journalism know, as Hunter S. Thompson said, "When the going gets weird, the weird turn pro."

CHAPTER 8

"WHEN THE GOING GETS WEIRD THE WEIRD TURN PRO."

As I think back on some of the experiences I had in Vietnam, they surprise even me, as does the fact that I handled them as well as I did. Some I self-inflicted because of stupidity or booze; others were merely chance.

If I were to encounter any one of these experiences today, I am sure they would sent me fleeing to a team of psychiatrists.

A SHAU VALLEY:

As I have mentioned, I was stationed by the A Shau Valley, a truly scary place. As was to be expected, it had been quickly nicknamed the Valley of Death. In fact, on my one photograph of the place that I brought home, someone had written Dante's admonition over the gates of hell: "Abandon All Hope, Ye Who Enter Here."

U.S. forces tried numerous times to go into that valley and set up bases, and never succeeded throughout the war.

One particularly gloomy day, I was flying in a chopper, high over the A Shau. The valley was encased in low, scudding clouds, and it presented a great shot for a picture. So I leaned out of the chopper to try and shoot a picture to capture this ominous sight.

There was a captain seated next to me, who had a headset on so he could hear what the pilots were saying. He finally tapped me on the shoulder and yelled into my ear, "I don't know if it makes a difference to you, but we are taking ground fire."

"Makes a difference! You damn right it makes a difference! Do I look like John Wayne here?"

Anyway, I pulled my idiot head into the chopper and got my helmet to sit on. There was a belief that sitting on your helmet might protect the family jewels if a round came up through the floor of the helicopter.

In retrospect, given that we were high over the A Shau, one of the few places I knew of where the NVA had higher caliber machine guns, in all likelihood we were seeing .50 caliber fire, and if a .50 caliber round came up through the floor and hit me, all my helmet would have done is provide additional shrapnel with which to turn me into a permanent soprano.

I never leaned out of another chopper.

One other time when I was flying high over the A Shau, I was with the commander of the Air Cav—an absolutely crazy bastard named Mannellini, I think. He used to show me his "Kill Board" with pride. "Look at this, Volk! There's not another unit in this AO (area of operation) that gets kills like this." Anyway, he was piloting a chopper, and again there was another officer seated next to me.

It was a great day, and we were so high it was actually chilly, which was nice. I was half asleep, when all of a sudden the power went completely off on the chopper. A helicopter with no power quickly went from being a flying machine to a rock. I have no idea how long the power was off, but it seemed like a long time as you begin to fall.

However, the power came back on, and that reassuring "whump, whump" of the blades returned. I was still filled with terror, and looked up at Colonel Mannellini in the pilot's seat, and he was laughing his ass off. The white-faced lieutenant next to me said, "He's just fucking around." My whole, short life had just passed in front of me and he was just fucking around? He was a weird person.

Choppers were so much a part of your life where I was stationed, since you could not go anywhere without them. There were damn few roads into triple canopy jungle.

As I mentioned, when dropping you off, most helicopters never landed, and you jumped when you got close to the ground. The only problem was, sometimes it was hard to tell where the ground was because of tall grasses, which the rotor blades would whip about.

I remember one time we were hovering and having a hard time telling our distance to "Mother Earth." Finally, someone jumped. I then heard the door gunner say to the pilot, "Cap, we need to hold up. That bastard's still falling." As it turns out he wasn't seriously hurt; however, he probably would have taken a broken bone or two.

In Vietnam everyone in the field dreamed of the "Million Dollar Injury," which was nothing more than getting hurt bad enough to get you sent to the rear, but not bad enough to really fuck you up.

I mostly flew in Hueys or LOHs, which were small observation helicopters, which I quite frankly enjoyed. Chinooks, huge double-bladed transport choppers, were a different story. They were called "Shithooks" for a reason. However, one time it was the most beautiful flying machine in the U.S. Army as I was trying to get off Firebase Barnett, the same place where a few other guys and I were given the gift of one soldier's last dehydrated onions.

New firebases, especially during the monsoon, were vulnerable places, and were quagmires of mud from all of the construction. Barnett had been under attack for some time, and we had been trying to clean the NVA out for weeks. However, whenever we went into this one ridge and fought them, they would quickly re-infiltrate once we left.

In fact, in the story I wrote on the building of Barnett, my lead read: "To the men of Co. B. 2nd Bn, 502nd Inf., it is called Comeback Ridge, but to the 71 North Vietnamese soldiers who died there, it would be more appropriately labeled Boot Hill East."

I was scheduled to get off the base; however, darkness and rain did not make it look likely. Finally, someone told me that one last Chinook was going to try and land, so I ran to the helipad.

Sure enough, this beautiful shit-hook came in low through the clouds and the mist headed for the base. "Please don't veer off, please don't veer off," were my only thoughts.

When it appeared he would land, I got as close to the pad as I could, because I knew he would not be on the ground long and wanted to be in a position to run on board. The result was me covered head to toe with red gumbo mud when the wash of the blades hit the ground. I ran on and sat down with a huge grin on my face, and then saw what had to be the "Cherriest Cherry" in all of Vietnam staring slack-jawed at me. I am sure he thought, "How can someone who looks so bad be so happy?"

When I got back to Camp Evans, I went to my hooch area and walked straight into a shower—weapon, clothes, and all. It was wonderful! In Vietnam you took your good fortune and joy where you found them.

EAGLE BEACH CRAZY:

Of all the experiences I had in Vietnam, none was crazier or potentially more dangerous than the one I had at Eagle Beach.

Eagle Beach was an in-country R&R (rest and relaxation) area for the 101st Airborne, located on a magnificent beach on the South China Sea. Occasionally line units would have a stand-down, whereby they would be brought to the rear to be re-fitted and given a break from the field.

It was a great place to relax, eat good food, drink, and for a while forget about the war.

However, like all other places where we operated, it had nothing that resembled women. Donut Dollies were sometimes there. ("Donut Dollies" were young ladies who worked for the Red Cross, I think, and they would go to the field from time to time dispensing writing materials, good cheer, and I suppose doughnuts.) However, at Eagle Beach they bikini-cavorted in the sand, dispensing nothing but hornied fantasies. Given that there were about 200 to 1 odds and all kinds of REMF officers, the chances of even getting close to these women was pretty remote, if not downright impossible.

This one particular time I was there with my favorite outfit, Charlie Company. A crazier bunch you would never find, and led by one of the true madmen of the war—a guy nicknamed Zippo 6, who I will cover more when we get to the characters section.

Anyway, two guys in this company and I had become good friends and had spent the afternoon drinking beer, badmouthing officers (except, of course, Zippo, who was loved by his men), and talking about sex. One of the group left for a while and then returned all excited.

He had learned that, in the small village by Eagle Beach, you could actually get some action, and better yet, one of the guys who was on guard duty at the road checkpoint leading out of the beach area was a buddy of his.

Well, faster then you can say "Boom-Boom," my two buddies—"Moe" and "Curly"—and I were off to find romance.

True to his word, he did know the guy at the checkpoint, and he let us through down the road to ville, which was fairly close. (This guard station on the road was a sandbagged affair with three guys and an M60 machine gun. It had concertina wire running off in both directions from the road, and I imagine there were other guard positions along the perimeter.)

Our luck continued to hold as we actually made contact with the "Slicky Boy," who apparently made the arrangements for this operation and who was accompanied by a number of "Slicky Boy" wannabees.

Now, I wasn't expecting a Saigon-type hotel complete with bar and restaurant, but what we got was weird beyond description. In essence, we were taken to an isolated location by a pagoda and then one at a time taken behind the pagoda.

Up to this point, things were a little hazy because of the amount of beer we had consumed, but I was sobering up fast and my lustful thoughts were quickly turning to: "This is dumb, this is really dumb." We didn't even have a weapon, for God's sake.

We went into the ville after this whole bizarre ordeal, had a few beers, and bought some tiger fatigues, which are nasty looking, tight-fitting uniforms. (I still have a picture of the three of us in our tiger fatigues. We are looking very serious and dangerous and my two buddies kind of pull it off. I, however, have these black horn-rimmed glasses, a very bad moustache, and a boony hat that has a Mexican sombrero look. Quite frankly, I look more like a bookkeeper for Pancho Villa then a lethal weapon of war.)

We also spoke with bravado about how we were probably the only soldiers at Eagle Beach to get laid that night. However, I sensed we were all just damn glad we were not killed for our boots and wallets.

We then headed on down the road. As we were approaching the open area that separated the tree line from the cleared field around Eagle Beach, something started nagging at me that I could not quite put my finger on. Something just did not feel right. Then all of a sudden it hit me! What if they had changed the guard while we were gone? What if my buddies' friend had been relieved and he had failed to tell the new shift that three idiots had gone into the ville?

I froze and told my companions to wait, and then I yelled, "We're from Charlie Company and we need to get back into the beach." We waited and then heard the guards yell back, "Who the hell are you?"

Damn, the guard had changed, and the soldiers who had known us had probably been replaced by some edgy cherries that at this very moment had their fingers on the M60 machine gun.

Now, we had been trained to look out for clever ruses that the NVA might use to get close to a position and then break through our perimeter. There was no password, as no one was supposed to be outside of the wire. I frantically searched my beer-soaked brain trying to think of some Americana trivia like they used in World War II to identify real Americans. "What town were the Dodgers in?" "What was Mae West's cup size?" But nothing came to mind.

What followed was a lot of ominous silence, and I thought, "Oh, God don't let me die at Eagle Beach for being dumb and sneaking into a ville to have a bad sexual encounter behind a pagoda."

However, it was too late for that crap, as my Catholic guilt had already kicked into overdrive and I knew in my heart that a couple of rounds from an M60 machine gun was probably exactly what I deserved for my transgressions.

Finally, my buddy yelled out the name of the guy who had let us through and told them to check with him if they didn't believe us. That seemed to do the trick, and we were allowed to approach very slowly with our hands up. Once our IDs were checked, we were allowed to re-enter Eagle Beach.

Over the years, through my stupidity—especially when mixed with alcohol—I am sure I have worked my guardian angel to a frazzle, but never more so than that night. I don't even want to think what might have happened if my tireless angel had not whispered in my ear, "What if they have changed the guard?"

There is kind of a weird postscript to some of the experiences I had, especially those where I put myself in harm's way.

While stupidity and booze are always a dangerous combination, especially in a war zone where everyone is walking around with guns, sometimes you never know what might come together to affect you in a place like Vietnam.

I have mentioned my buddy Harmon, who was currently living in Saigon in the hotel by the whorehouse—the same Harmon who had led us astray on the Vietnam rotation schedule back at DINFOs and caused me to blow off White House Communication, and who had caused us all to get Article 15s back at Oakland.

Well, for some reason known only to him, he decided to leave cushy Saigon and travel north to see his country cousins. So he picked up Ortiz in Da Nang, and they arrived at my base camp north of Hue. As humble as it was, our Enlisted Men's Club was soon the site of an all-night party between old friends.

The next morning, Harmon and Ortiz left, and I—with my massive hangover—headed to the helipad, which would take me to a firebase. However, due to my partying I missed the first helicopter. My buddy, who ran the operation, took one look at me and said, "Volk, you are one lucky son-of-a-bitch. The eight a.m. chopper you were supposed to have been on took fire, and we had two WIAs." Don't ask me to explain it, but somehow drinking and hanging out with "Black Cloud" Harmon had saved me from making the eight a.m. chopper, which had then been shot up. Sometimes life was just too weird.

FIREBASE TOMAHAWK:
I think there is a time and place for every soldier at war when he passes from being a very frightened, edgy participant to someone who becomes desensitized and dispassionate.

I am sure my transformation came on Firebase Tomahawk. Quite frankly, it was a relatively safe firebase, which is why I did not mind spending time there.

We were set up for the night, and I was in a bunker on the perimeter. A firebase, by the way, was a forward position for artillery and essentially was created by chopping the top of a hill and then clearing all trees and foliage for some distance around that hill position. We then encircled the entire thing with concertina wire, claymores, foo gas (barrels filled with aviation fuel, which when detonated spewed fire forward), trip flares, etc.

Anyway, we thought we heard movement through much of the night, and thought we might be getting probed by sappers (very cool NVA soldiers who could slither and slide their way through all kinds of obstacles without making a sound).

If sappers actually breached your perimeter, they could cause all kinds of problems with their satchel charges (explosives), and would create such confusion and havoc we would have as likely shot each other as them.

However, if for any reason they were discovered coming up the hill with no cover, they were, as we would say, SOL (shit out of luck). That is what happened to these sappers; as one of them tripped a flare on the concertina wire and then all hell broke lose.

Our side of the fight is relatively easy, as we just pulled the pins on grenades and rolled them down the hill. (It is interesting, as we always used to piss and moan about having to lug boxes of grenades down to the bunkers on the perimeter.)

This fight went on until almost dawn, but in the end there were twenty-one dead NVA, which when collected were stacked like cordwood on top of a net, which at some point a Chinook helicopter picked up and hauled to a mass grave.

It wasn't during the fight that I knew I had gone through the transformation that I talked about earlier; it was my reaction when I saw twenty-one dead young men piled up. I would have expected myself to be shocked or repulsed, but I wasn't. I don't even remember feeling "Better them than us." I was at most mildly curious, but ambivalent comes most to mind.

I don't know if I knew I had changed at the time, but in looking back now it is most obvious. When someone like me can walk by that type of carnage and view the bodies of twenty-one men, who had families, loved ones, and wanted desperately to enjoy life, and not feel any emotion stronger than ambivalence, I had most definitely been transformed.

LAST MAN OFF RIPCORD:

Unlike Tomahawk, which as I said was always considered a fairly safe firebase, Firebase Ripcord was just the opposite. It was hell and gone out into the boonies, was hard to re-supply—especially in the monsoon—was always getting shelled, and—this will sound strange—but just seemed to have a bad feel to it.

I did not like it and I had a feeling it did not like me, which probably explains what happened.

On most firebases we would do a last light and first light sweep of the area around the base, mainly to see that everything was set up OK and that claymores were in place and properly hooked up. (Sappers were so good they would sometimes turn our claymores around, and when we pulled the clacker, or trigger, the claymores would fire on us.)

Anyway, these were fairly routine and not considered any big deal. I was on a first light sweep one time on Ripcord and not watching where I was going. I got too close to the top of the firebase, where the 155mm cannons were. (155s were big ass cannons.) The cannon fired and the concussion knocked me off my feet and dazed me. Now, when I came to I just knew that I had set off an unexploded grenade or something and that I was in shock (which explained the absence of pain) and that I was badly wounded.

So I refused to open my eyes (I didn't want to see the wreckage) and tentatively started feeling my extremities, beginning with my crotch because, as I have noted, this was a fairly important item to us boys. The next thing I heard was gales of laughter coming from the guys I was with, and when I finally realized I was OK and opened my eyes, there stood my buddies, with their eyes shut and holding their crotches. Of course I started to laugh, both out of relief and the fact that a guy with his eyes shut, holding his crotch, is probably pretty funny. However, going from being seriously wounded to laughter in a matter of seconds is a strange experience.

Ripcord, by the way, was finally overrun, and I was luckily not present. It was under siege for weeks, and during that time we lied like crazy to the civilian press boys when they kept asking about another Khe Sahn in the making.

After it finally fell, there were claims from at least one hundred GIs that they were the last man off Ripcord. As it turned out, the last man off Ripcord was a South Vietnamese soldier who hid the entire night while the NVA rummaged through the base. After they left, he left.

Thereafter, whenever someone would start in about some John Wayne exploits, we would reference him as also being "the last man off Ripcord."

REST AND RELAXATION—R&R:

There was something strange about leaving a war to take a week's vacation in Hawaii. I know soldiers, especially frontline soldiers from other wars, were given leaves so they could get a break from the fighting; however, Vietnam took that to a whole new level. Everyone got a week's vacation to any number of exotic places all over the world.

You could also take a week's leave later in your tour, and I was set to go to Australia at the end of my tour; however, I got a drop of almost a month, which meant my tour was shortened. This was under Nixon's phony sham called Vietnamization.

Next to DEROS (going home), there was nothing as important as your week of R&R; however, as I remember, the schedule did not permit any leeway. If your R&R ran from August 8-15, those were your days, and if something happened to delay you the clock still started running on the eighth. I went during the monsoon season, which made sunny Hawaii sound even more inviting. However, because of the weather, chopper service between Camp Evans and Da Nang, where I would fly out of, was always uncertain.

For that reason, I decided I would not rely on a chopper but would hitchhike down to Da Nang and stay with my marine buddy Sergio Ortiz over the weekend and fly out of Da Nang on Sunday. (This gives you some idea of how secure the lowlands were during this time. Outside of a few danger spots like the Hi Van Pass, hitchhiking along Highway 1 was safer than a lot of places in the States.)

My idea of going early was a good plan, for you did not want to be standing on a monsoon-soaked tarmac somewhere in Vietnam when your R&R started. The only faulty part of this scheme, however, is that I had forgotten how totally crazy Ortiz was. The next thing I knew, I was screaming toward the Da Nang Press Club in a pickup that Ortiz said he had "borrowed" from the navy. I should mention that, because of some problems that the 101st Airborne Division apparently caused when they first went to Vietnam, everywhere—and I mean everywhere, except our area of operation—was off limits to us.

The night at the press club is a little hazy; however, I do remember Sergio standing up at one point and announcing, "When Ortiz drinks, everybody drinks. Set 'em up for the house!" He then sat down and whispered to me, "Volk, you got any money?" Thank God drinks were cheap and the crowd was small.

It was during the trip back to the marine barracks when I started to sober up and consider my precarious situation. Here we were, a marine—who I am sure did not have a scrap of paper authorizing him to be where he was—and an army guy from the 101st Airborne, who was off limits everywhere. And, to make matters even worse, Sergio had driven too close to an ARVN deuce-and-a-half (a large transport truck) and smashed the rearview mirror, so that now our borrowed navy pickup was a damaged navy pickup.

We somehow found our way to the checkpoint at the marine base, and we were so close to making it I could almost taste the mai tai's on Waikiki Beach. The checkpoint had one of those portable stop signs in the middle of the road and a marine off to the side checking Vietnamese civilians into the camp. (I forgot to mention it was dawn by this time.)

Ortiz eased up to the checkpoint and hit and knocked over the portable stop sign. I swear to God he knocked over this guy's portable stop sign! The marine guard headed over to us and began shaking his head about halfway there. Oahu was looking very far away.

However, Sergio actually talked his way through this mess. I have already mentioned that, as marine bullshitters went, Ortiz was in a class of his own.

So we began to slowly drive away, and when we had gotten about ten feet, Sergio stopped the pickup and yelled out the window: "What?" I looked back, and the marine wasn't even looking at us, let alone talking to us; although he did turn around and begin to head our way. By this time my nerves were frayed, and I yelled, "Ortiz, drive this vehicle away from here right now or you are the next KIA of this fucking war!"

What little sleep I got after that was filled with nightmares of me calling Susan and explaining that I might be a little late arriving in Hawaii, as I was currently in a marine brig in Da Nang.

The week in Hawaii with Susan was nice. Hot showers, making love, good food, sleeping, and the absence of danger were all a tonic. Like all such things, it went too fast. However, even during that time we spent together in Oahu, I sensed a change between us. Or, more accurately, a change in me. She had gone back to live with her parents while I was away, so she hadn't changed a bit. I, on the other hand, had gone off to war, and there is no way that does not change you very deeply.

I DO BELIEVE THAT MAN IS SHOOTING AT ME:
The other occurrence which I believe signaled that I was becoming somewhat desensitized to the war came when I was returning from R&R. I had just spent a wonderful week in sunny Hawaii and was greeted by more damn rain back in Vietnam.

This prevented me from getting back to Camp Evans, so I spent the night in Phu Bai with a captain whom I had met on the plane. He was a veterinarian in the "World," which of course led the U.S. Army to make him a food inspector.

He was a very bright, Hawkeye Pierce type and obviously did not have any problem putting up a lowly Specialist Four like me.

Between the rain and just returning from loved ones in Hawaii, we decided to have a drink; however, the only thing he had was two bottles of Drambuie. We proceeded to drink both, and if someone would have recorded our conversation most of the world's problems would have been solved as we solved them that night.

Now, I don't know how many of you have drunk much Drambuie, but it is a wonderful, heavy, Scotch-based liqueur that is great in small amounts after dinner. In large amounts, it is lethal.

Of course, the Good Lord, in order to remind Catholic boys what happens when you overindulge, made sure the weather prevented me from catching a helicopter and I was directed to a deuce-and-a-half (2.5 ton) truck. Now, normally this would not have been a problem; however, on this particular day I could not even fit my head into my helmet, which is not how you want to ride in this truck, as they were built totally and unequivocally without anything that resembled a shock absorber. I kid you not, it was made of steel, and a pebble in the road would send a bone-jarring shock into you.

It was getting dark by the time we left, and to make this whole ordeal even worse, my driver was a pot head who would light up a joint just as soon as we cleared Phu Bai camp and cranked up his boom box, which was playing "Inna Godda Da Vida" as loud as it would go.

So between this blaring music hitting my head like a hammer, the sickening sweet smell of marijuana, the deuce-and-a-half which treats every small bump like it was a bomb crater, and the worst hangover in Southeast Asia, I proceed to stick my head out of the window like a dog in a pickup.

The only thought in my pain-wracked body was of the Lakota Indians in my home state of South Dakota, who used to have a saying that "It is a good day to die."

Not a thought you should probably have in a war zone, because as I looked out into the pitch-dark night I could see green tracers coming out of a tree line zooming behind us. Now, I could not hear anything because of all the noise in the truck, but I could tell a couple of things: First, this guy in the tree line was not leading us near enough as we were barreling along. Second, he was firing something other than an AK-47, as the rate of fire was so slow.

I quickly looked over at my wasted driver and realized that he probably didn't know what country we were in, let alone that we were taking fire from a tree line.

I looked back and still saw the green tracers flying toward us, but still far to our rear. I made the decision quickly that I wasn't going to say anything unless that horrible sharpshooter, Nuyen MaGoo, over in that tree line, started to get a lot closer to the truck. It was my considered opinion that if I shocked Specialist "Stoned" out of his reverie with the news we were taking fire, he would in all likelihood panic and immediately drive the deuce-and-a-half into the ditch, killing us both.

We were quickly past that area, and I sat back and thought of what had just transpired. Someone had been shooting at us, and I had just watched it as if I were at a movie. How strange things had become, as I have a sense that if someone were to shoot at me today my reaction would be different.

I have to say that I even felt a little better after the whole incident. My driver wasn't a bad guy—strange in that way most guys from motor pools were, but not bad. "Inna Godda Da Vida" didn't seem as grating, and took on kind of a nice, surreal sound as we sped down Highway 1. Even the old deuce-and-a-half seemed to ride better.

When we got back to Camp Evans, my driver dropped me off and I was just about to tell him what had transpired, but then thought, "Why? Why ruin this guy's evening?" So I thanked him and wished him well.

Dr. Hunter S. Thompson had been oh so right: "When the going had gotten weird, the weird had turned pro."

CHAPTER 9

ASSORTED FRUITS AND NUTS: "Piss Willy" to "Joe the Shit Man."

I think the shock I experienced dealing with some of the strange characters and menagerie of people that made up my army experiences was even greater for someone like me, who had been plucked from the heartland where diversity and culture clashes generally involved a German Catholic marrying a Norwegian Lutheran.

The first character I want to describe wasn't even a person but a dog: "Piss Willy."

Dogs were very prevalent in large camps like Evans. They provided companionship to GIs a long way from home and seemed to be everywhere. The only problem that I observed was that these camps had been around for a long time, and by 1970 the amount of inbreeding among these dogs had reached a serious level. This gene pool had no deep end.

The result of this was some very strange, spooky, mutant mutts. I'm talking Stephen King scary. Dogs with huge bodies and tiny legs, weird tails and ears, etc. If they weren't physically affected, I had a sense most of them were mentally unbalanced—some of them in a mean, crazy sort of way.

However, one dog had none of these mental or physical problems. He was a terrific dog named "Piss Willy." However, over the years—perhaps because of a lost love or the strain of war—Piss Willy had become a drunk. Not just your run-of-the-mill ordinary drunk, but a great drunk. He could find a hooch party faster then Lassie could find Timmy in the well. There he would be an honored guest with everyone buying him beer. In fact, it was considered a good sign if Piss Willy deigned to show up for your DEROS party (Date Expected, Return Overseas).

Although a small dog, he was also tough and resilient. I once opened a hooch door that had six steep wooden steps. Unfortunately, Piss Willy had passed out on the top stair and he went rolling down these steps. I was sure I had killed him, as he never made a sound. However, once he hit the ground he picked himself up, gave me a bleary-eyed glare, and staggered off to find a safer place to sleep it off.

At the other end of the dog spectrum were two dogs called Bitch and Bastard. They had to be two of the most mean-spirited, psychotic dogs on the planet.

My friend who owned them lived in a hooch right behind mine, and when you got close to our compound you automatically picked up rocks, as these two nasty curs would come snapping and snarling at you.

They were constantly having litters, and would use the space between the ground and our hooch floor to deliver, and would come snapping out whenever you walked by. I never saw any pups, and don't even want to think about that.

My buddy finally went home, and all of us promised we would take care of his beloved dogs after he was gone. Fat chance! That guy had not even cleared division headquarters when two of his hooch mates loaded up Bitch and Bastard, drove them out of the gate, threw some meat into the ditch, and when the greedy mutts went to get it proceeded to send them both to their just rewards, where I am sure they are hounds of hell right now.

It was never lost on me that two dogs, aptly named Bitch and Bastard, ended up dead in a ditch, while a lovable drunk called Piss Willy was the toast of the town.

I should note that the dogs also provided some diversion to bored soldiers in the rear. They were constantly screwing and were the only animals in a place like Camp Evans who got any real action. However, like everything else that involved these mental misfits, their lovemaking was always preceded by some nasty, ménage à trois, snarling fight, after which some poor loser would be run off. We always bet on them and rather enjoyed the show.

I know that kind of voyeurism sounds crass, and I was always surprised to find how quickly men with no women around could get back to a very base nature. I don't mean to get too philosophical here, but it is true. It reminded me to some degree of my own state's history, which early on was settled mostly by men. It was an environment of violence, lawlessness, and crude living for many years. We men made a total mess of things until enough women rolled out of the east to take us by our collective ears and make us build schools, churches, and such.

Interestingly enough, I never saw Piss Willy engage in any of this fighting or fucking. I guess all of his energy and will was devoted to his one great vice—Demon Rum.

POP:

The human equivalent to Piss Willy was a wonderful old drunk who had to be the oldest corporal in the army, whom everyone called Pop. I have no idea what his age was, but he looked as if he had been in the military since the Punic Wars.

Every night Pop would come into the Enlisted Men's Club and regale us young soldiers with tales of the army long past.

By 1970 he had served countless tours in Vietnam and had no desire to return stateside. Given his age and rank, I would surmise he was like my marine buddy Janklow, who used to say, "Ya, I made lance corporal, three times."

I once asked Garza, who ran the clubs, what would possess someone who looked to be one hundred years old to hang around Vietnam. Garza said, "Volk, look at him. He sits here every night, drinks for free, tells his stories, and is the lovable Pop. Back home he is just an aging soldier who probably gets bounced from the army and ends up a town drunk somewhere. No, when this war is over so is Pop."

Anyway, he was a wonderful old guy, and I loved his tales. I am sure Pop has long since gone to that big NCO club in the sky. If so, I hope he is sitting around, drinking beer and sharing his wonderful stories with soldiers from other wars and other times.

THE MEXICAN MAFIA:

One thing a person learns very quickly in Vietnam is that, in addition to the normal supply lines that took care of our daily needs, there was also a sub-rosa system that operated almost totally on the ancient barter system.

This economic structure provided the little niceties and delicacies not normally available to GIs like me. Now, I am not talking about booze, cigarettes, or drugs, which were not only in large supply but were also incredibly cheap. What I am referring to were things like steaks, Long Range Patrol Packets (LRPs, which I mentioned earlier), electric fans (incredibly valuable especially in summer and always in short supply), and almost anything else that was hard to get and which made your life a little easier or even pleasant.

Senior NCOs mainly conducted this underground, and by far the best at it was Sergeant Garza, who operated both the Enlisted Men's Club and the Senior NCO Club. Sarge had strategically-placed fellow Mexican soldiers in every location where supplies came into the camp. This group he lovingly called his "Mexican Mafia." It was not unusual for us to be eating steak, fresh eggs, and potatoes when the rest of the camp was eating Shit on a Shingle.

He was a great guy, generous to a fault with his friends and, in addition to being one hell of an operator in the barter sub-world, was a hell of a poker player. His games at the Senior NCO Club were legendary.

Now, I played small-stakes poker at my hooch with my buddies, but only got into one of Garza's big games once. I was quickly gutted by a fat Filipino from the USO, who hit a straight flush that beat my full house. I sat numbly (much like Steve McQueen in the "The Cincinnati Kid") as I watched a month's pay fly away to Manila.

Now, most of Sarge's Mexican Mafia were friendly, easygoing types; however, there was one who was as scary a guy as I was to meet in the army. His unlikely nickname was Rabbit.

It is hard for me to describe now what made him seem so dangerous, but it was there. A cold, quiet, threatening air.

Even when he became indebted to me, he still made me nervous. This indebtedness came about one night when a buddy and I were out taking a leak into the ditch that ran by the EM Club. Across the street was a transportation group and, as I already noted, motor pool people were just plain crazy.

These guys were always fighting, raising hell, doing drugs, and popping smoke (grenades that showed different color smoke to show helicopters your situation in the field).

Anyway, this night we heard and saw smoke get popped over at the motor pool. It was a perfectly still night, and we watched this smoke drift over to us. As it got near, my buddy Sam, Sam the Wounded Man said, "What if that is not smoke but CS?"—a very nasty tear gas. These words were no sooner out of his mouth then the gas hit us. We went tearing into the club, yelling for everyone to get out, but it was too late—and by the time we got out back our eyes were watering and we were spitting up and gasping for breath. All of a sudden I realized that Rabbit was not with us but was still in the club as he had passed out in the bar. Back in I went and got him out.

From then on he was my ever-present protector. He gave me his Zippo lighter, which read, "When I die, I know I will go to heaven because I have spent my time in Hell—Phu Bai, Vietnam." However, it wasn't enough for Rabbit.

One night when someone was giving me a hard time I looked over, and there sat Rabbit staring at this guy with the most predatory look I have ever seen. Garza saw it too and immediately steered the guy away. Like I said, he was one scary guy.

The Mexican Mafia was truly a well-oiled machine, and if the rest of our war effort had been run with the efficiency and skill of Garza and his amigos, the war would have been over in months, not years.

JUICE:
Some people had power and status merely by virtue of the jobs they held. It was called "juice." The guy who handled your mail was one of these. Anytime I saw my mailman, I never failed to buy him a beer and compliment him on the great job he was doing. You piss off your mail guy and the next thing you know you're not getting any mail, and your R&R orders have mysteriously been delivered to Pvt. Van Tran Dong of the 43rd North Vietnamese Regiment.

In the days before e-mail, cell phones, etc., mail was critically important to a soldier in Vietnam, and a care package, or pictures from home, could make your whole week. One of the most endearing things my ex-wife Susan ever did for me was to write every day I was in Vietnam so that I never went a day without mail. I hope I remembered to thank her for that.

I even had a moment in the sun of the underground world of barter and "juice." A U.S. Air Force guy had been transferred to Camp Evans from division headquarters at Eagle. His mail, however, was still going to Eagle. Because I traveled down there a lot, as a favor I started picking up his mail for him, or arranged to have it picked up.

One day he came in and handed me a package and said, "These are yours for one week." Inside were two 16mm reel-to-reel dirty movies. For one week I was the most popular guy at Evans. Young captains and lieutenants came into our PIO hooch asking for "Mr. Volk." Ah, for one brief shining moment.

JOE "THE SHIT MAN."
Joe "The Shit Man" had not been as fortunate as me, and after completing basic training had been sent to that dreaded place 11 Bravo, and there was taught the art of war as an infantryman. After that, he was promptly sent to Vietnam as a grunt.

However, unlike most line soldiers, the first time bullets started whizzing over his head Joe had a revelation. Now, I am not talking about some subtle whisper in his ear. No, this was a revelation on the nature of Saul on the road to Damascus, and it screamed to him: "JOE, YOU'RE A PACIFIST!"

While the army condoned and almost encouraged the old dictum that "there are no atheists in a foxhole," battlefield conversions to pacifism were something they did not take kindly to.

You start letting frontline GIs discover that they are in reality conscientious objectors, and the next thing you know there is an exodus to the rear that becomes epidemic.

Hell, too much of that kind of attitude across the globe and peace could break out.

So to discourage these types of battlefield epiphanies, the army would bust the offending soldier to the lowest rank possible, impose other military penalties, and finally give that person the worst job in the camp.

Now, the worst job in a large camp like Evans was burning shit. I have already mentioned that we had no indoor plumbing and that we used plywood outhouses equipped with fifty-gallon drums cut in half.

You have a couple thousand soldiers using these types of facilities, and obviously someone has to come along and pick up the cans and dispose of it. "Honey Dippers" who had this job used a small-motorized platform vehicle called a "Mule," and they would take the barrel halves to the edge of the base and pour gasoline over the offal and burn it, and it was this job that Joe found himself doing once he discovered his passive side.

I am sure it would have been easy for Joe to resent this type of treatment, hate the army for not respecting his divine revelation, and despise his job; however, nothing could be farther from the truth. Everywhere he went on his little mule he waved to the passersby and had, if you will excuse the expression, a big shit-eating grin on his face.

I once asked him why he was so happy all the time given his employment, and he looked at me and said, "Volk, no one has taken a shot at me in weeks."

No amount of ribbing could dissuade him from infectious good humor. Sometimes, when we would be having a beer, Joe would say shit about something and someone would invariably say, "Joe, don't talk shop while we're at the club." Didn't matter to Joe, and he continued to make his appointed rounds with joy and élan.

There are those who would say that Joe "The Shit Man" was a coward, but I never felt that way about him and always took him at his word. In many respects he probably did more for the war effort then a lot of officers I knew. He was a good guy and my friend, who took the worst job imaginable and did it with good humor and style.

There is an old saying that "If life hands you lemons you should make lemonade." Well, life handed Joe shit, and he made a fine fertilizer from it.

LIEUTENANT BERRY:

There truly was a mixed bag of crazies, eccentrics, and operators that I met while in Vietnam. One of the many books I read during that time was Joseph Heller's wickedly funny *Catch-22*. Talk about life imitating art.

I swear there were countless characters that were the spitting image of people in his novel. Majors who were never available: Major-Major, Ex-PFC Wintergreen, entrepreneurs, and even one gung-ho lieutenant who I swear was just like the STRAC lieutenant in *Catch-22*, who wanted to bolt the soldiers together so they would march in a more rigid formation.

However, all that being said, I should also mention one of the most decent and honorable men I served with. His name was 2nd Lieutenant Berry, and he commanded our Public Information Office at Camp Evans.

He was a Mormon from Utah and a gentleman in every sense of the word, whose only goal was getting everyone safely home. (You would think that was a fairly common goal, but you could not believe how some officers exposed their men to unnecessary risk especially when it did not include them putting their own butts on the line.)

Although he did not smoke or drink I never saw him judge others who did. He had a causal manner with us but got more stories from his brigade then any others because of how he led.

He had a great sense of humor, and once when he was getting ready to go on R&R brought his lieutenant's cap in with its butter bar on it and hung it in the office and told us that in his absence we could salute his hat every morning.

This from a guy who never wanted a salute from anyone.

Interestingly enough, when he was leaving to go home, he came over to my hooch to take a picture of me. I had been nursing a bad ankle after a clumsy entry into a bunker during a rocket attack. After he took the picture, he turned to go and I said, "Lieutenant," and when he turned back I gave him the only salute I ever willingly delivered to an officer.

In a bad place he was an island of decency and goodness and honor, and I so hope he has had a good life.

ZIPPO 6:

Because of my job as a correspondent and combat photographer, I traveled with many different infantry companies during my tour. Without a doubt the most capable and charismatic company commander I would meet was Captain Mark Smith, call sign Zippo 6.

He had acquired his name in a previous tour during search-and-destroy missions down in the delta, when villages were burned and their inhabitants relocated.

The fire of choice: the ever-reliable Zippo lighter.

It was my experience that the men in most companies did not have a very high opinion of their officers and questioned their competency. There was a saying that the most dangerous thing in Vietnam was a second lieutenant with a compass.

Not Zippo's men. They idolized their flamboyant captain, who walked with a swagger and carried a heavy cane that he used to tap you with to get your attention. He humped an NVA rucksack, carried an AK 47, and called everyone rookie.

He was in his third tour when I met him. He had been an enlisted man before getting a field grade commission from

Westmoreland during the huge communist offensive of TET in 1968. I always felt that was one of the reasons he treated his men so well—because he had once been one of them.

He commanded, in my opinion, the most dangerous unit in the 101st Airborne—Charlie Company.

He used to deride the other companies for the hardcore names they would bestow on themselves. Any time we would be in the battalion area at our base camp, he would point out the other company's signs, "Look at the bullshit Rookie; Ass Kicking Alpha; Battling Bastards of Bravo. We only have one name for my company, and we don't put it on no fucking sign—Chopping Charlie."

This, he confided to me, was because of the practice of chopping the ears off their kills—supposedly to keep their souls from entering the afterlife, or some such thing.

Zippo had one rule of engagement when he made contact: obliterate everything at his front. While we were trained to fire our M16s on semi-automatic, Zippo's men always fired Rock and Roll fully automatic. When he got into a firefight he would call in artillery, Cobra helicopter gunships, and Phantom jets if he could get them.

He turned everything to his front into a wasteland, including any unfortunate enemy soldiers who happened to be there.

Now, I don't know how good the NVA intelligence was, but I always had a sense that they knew of Zippo and Charlie Company and tried to avoid them. He never seemed to make as much contact as other companies in the same AO (area of operation).

For that reason I traveled with Charlie Company whenever I could. If the NVA wanted to avoid Zippo that was fine with me, as I sure as hell wanted to avoid them.

I got permission to write an article on Zippo and his incredible career for our magazine *Rendezvous With Destiny*. While I was working on it, Zippo, who was nearing the end of his tour, went on his last patrol. A low-risk affair into the lowlands using a jeep and two deuce-and-a-halfs to haul his men.

However, like his whole career, nothing was ever simple or uneventful, not even the end. His company actually found and killed an NVA soldier hiding in a spider hole.

Now, rather than just leave the dead soldier for someone else to pick up, Zippo proceeded to tie him to the front of his jeep, and with his company in tow he drove through the streets of Hue on his way back to Evans.

While the locals thought this great and cheered enthusiastically, the army brass up the feeding chain had a much different take on the event.

A few days later, Zippo came down to my PIO hooch and asked to see the article. I gave it to him, and after reading it, he looked up and said, "That reads real good, Rookie. When will it run?"

I was stunned, and said, "Zippo, are you crazy? This article is not only DOA at battalion and brigade headquarters, it is DOA at division. Hell, the bastards at MACV Saigon have probably waded in on killing it. After your stunt in Hue the other day, you, sir, are persona non grata."

He slowly shook his head and said, "That's the problem with the world today, Rook: no sense of style."

I have often wondered what happened to soldiers like Zippo and others like him. Zippo loved war, and the adrenaline rush of combat was an addictive drug.

Back home, if he stayed in the army, he would be Captain Mark Smith—an unorthodox, irreverent troublemaker. However, in the jungles of Vietnam he was Zippo 6—a very dangerous young man.

I was to meet other soldiers like Zippo, men who in some strange way had become addicted to war and combat. It is a strange phenomenon, and one I was even going to battle a little upon my return.

One person in particular I remember was a guy called Lucky, who was a Ranger, and who I met when I did the article on them.

I have no idea how many tours he had done; however, whenever he was rotated stateside, he could not get back to Vietnam fast enough. I once asked him what he would do once the war ended, and he answered that he would become a mercenary somewhere. Unfortunately, he would never get that chance, as his luck ran out on Firebase Ripcord a few months later.

CHAPTER 10

I DON'T MEAN TO GET OFF ON A RANT HERE.

I was fortunate during the eleven months I was in Vietnam not to lose a friend that I was really close to. However, there was a death of an acquaintance that affected me in a number of different ways. I am ashamed to say I cannot even remember his name or his nickname, which everyone had in Vietnam.

He mostly worked at our DTOC (Division Tactical Operations Center) monitoring sensing devices we would put out into the jungle. These instruments could detect movement and came in the shape of dog turds, branches, etc.

I used to go over to the DTOC and visit with him, and he would show me his sensor screens, and I remember one time he said, "Volk, look at this movement right here. This is a free-fire zone, so this has to be NVA." (Free-fire zones were places where supposedly there were no friendly or civilian people and we were free to fire.)

I asked him why we didn't fire on them, and he replied that ever since the My Lai massacre we would not fire on anything for which we did not make visual confirmation, even if they were in a free-fire zone.

A few weeks later I got off a chopper at the base camp late one afternoon, and my friend was going out on a last sweep of the perimeter before dark. He asked me to wait on dinner for him and we would go together. As I mentioned, last and first light sweeps of the perimeter was generally a boring, low-risk task.

Two and half hours later I was still waiting and finally decided to go to dinner, pissed off, thinking he had forgotten or found a better deal. It was at the mess hall that I learned that my buddy had tripped a booby trap and was dead.

I don't know why this depressed me so much, for he wasn't that close, but I think it had something to do with the incident at the DTOC when he identified NVA soldiers on his screen and told me we could not fire on them because of an incident that happened years before.

I kept wondering if those enemy soldiers that we had failed to deal with were the ones who set the booby trap for my friend.

The war was truly getting crazy by 1970, being totally driven by the political situation back home. Kent State had occurred, and it was obvious that the anti-war movement was going to start driving our policy.

I have to say that when I heard about Kent State it was truly one of the most depressing days of my life. Young people were dying in this God-awful war, while at home guardsmen had killed college students at Kent State. The world just didn't seem to be making any sense.

I guess what made Vietnam so crazy and depressing was that, by 1970 at least, everyone—from Buck Private "Joe The Shit Man" to General Creighton Abrams to everyone in the White House—knew the war was lost.

Without constant, massive American support the ARVNs were never going to be a match for the NVA, and with things going as they were back home that constant support would not be there.

However, the war would go on for another five years and over 10,000 more Americans would die. All for some asinine slogan like "Peace With Honor."

I am not using some thirty-year-old hindsight here. The absolute truth is, everyone by 1970 knew the war was lost, and not one of us was the least bit surprised when the North

Vietnamese conquered the south in a matter of months once we had left. We were just upset that we hadn't, as someone once said, "declared victory and gone home" many years before.

The war was probably lost, and people in power, knew it was lost, prior to 1970. A lot of people think that it became a lost cause after the "Tet Media Offensive" of 1968. Shortly after Tet, Walter Cronkite made his famous commentary on how our leaders were misleading us with false hope, that we were bogged down and probably would not win. It was reported that after President Johnson saw that broadcast, he said: "If I've lost Cronkite, I've lost the war." LBJ bailed out two months later, shocking the nation by announcing that he would not seek re-election. At that point, the president and I had something in common; we both knew when our tours of duty would end.

Beyond all that, and certainly by 1970, when Vietnamization was being implemented, we knew it was a strategy of deception. It had no chance of keeping the NVA from overrunning the South once our boots were off the ground.

I spent a good deal of time reporting on the training of the Regional and Provincial forces. (We called them Ruff and Puff's.) Under Vietnamization, they would take over for the Army of the Republic of Vietnam (ARVN) in protecting the lowlands. That would allow the ARVN to take our place in the jungle. Most of the time, we doubted which side the "Ruff and Puffs" were really on. Even if (and perhaps when) they were on our side, tiger-blooded defenders of Jeffersonian democracy they were not. On their best day, they would have proved no match for a determined Cub Scout troop from Sioux Falls, SD.

I guess it is the only thing I am truly bitter about after all these years—that so many wonderful American soldiers were allowed to die when everyone knew we would not win. For some reason I think of those young men more today than I once did and have a profound sense of sadness that so many died when the war was lost.

(I want to add here that I have this same sense of dread for our current war in Iraq. That it is lost, and yet we will stubbornly stay and lose more American lives. I have talked to a number of veterans of the Iraq war, both enlisted men and officers, and every one of them say the same thing: that, regardless of whether we stay six weeks or six years more, Iraq will hopelessly erupt into civil war and democracy will die a quick death there.)

However, these were not thoughts I had at the end of 1970 when I was visiting with Joe The Bartender and someone came in and said the Red Cross guy was looking for me. Understand: Unless your wife was pregnant, you did not want to hear that the Red Cross guy was looking for you. He was invariably the harbinger of bad news. Not this time, as he told me my drop (going home early) had come through. I was going home!

CHAPTER 11

"THERE'S NO PLACE LIKE HOME; THERE'S NO PLACE LIKE HOME."

As I already noted, taking off from Cam Rahn Bay and banking out over the South China Sea on my way home was a memorable moment.

The rest of the trip was pretty much like the journey over—long, tiring, and smelly, although I do remember that the flight attendants brought us hot towels for our faces. Funny how such a small act of kindness can be remembered all these years later.

The only other thing that sticks out was when, after countless hours on the plane, the pilot came on the intercom and said, "Gentlemen, we have just crossed over the continental United States of America."

The cheer that went up in that miserable airplane I am sure could be heard on the ground. Our elation, however, was to be short-lived.

We landed in Seattle and, like Seattle is most of the time, it was raining. It was the middle of the night, and we wearily got off the plane. (There was a rumor that they brought us home in the middle of the night so we would be spared problems with war protestors.)

What a grand feeling that left us all with. We had just spent a year serving our country overseas, and now were being sneaked back into that country like thieves in the night, to protect us from our own citizens.

Once off the plane we huddled on the runway, being held up for some reason. Finally, some sleepy clerk came out and gave us all small tickets, like you used to get at the movies. He told us we could walk over to this mess hall and get a steak with the ticket.

Now, since we were the only ones who would be in this mess hall at 3 a.m., why the army had to hold us up in the rain to give us tickets is beyond me. Just the army being the army, I guess.

We began to trudge over to the mess hall, and as we got close we passed under a big sign that read: "WELCOME HOME, JOB WELL DONE." Ah, the appreciation of a grateful nation. The first few guys silently raised their middle fingers as they went through, and all of us followed suit. No one said a word.

I have a sense that we all thought: "You can take your 'Welcome Home, Job Well Done' sign and put it where the sun doesn't shine."

Things get a little hazy after that. I do remember the steak was bad. My friend Suderman and I finally ended up in a bar at the Seattle airport, where we were going to celebrate our homecoming. We managed one beer before fatigue took over, so we headed for a makeshift room that I think was run by the USO.

In this room there were bunk beds that ran three high. It was managed by a sweet, grandmotherly lady who motherhenned this huge room of sleepy GIs. Once she found out when we had to wake up to catch our flight, she put our shoes into little slipper pouches that hung on the end of our beds. There was a paper clock face, also at the end of the bed, and she set this to correspond to when we had to get up. Once again a small act of kindness and care was greatly appreciated and remembered.

The only vivid memory I have of the trip from Seattle to Sioux Falls is getting on a rather small plane in Rapid City, which made a stop in our state capital of Pierre.

The plane was chock full of drunken revelers headed for Pierre and the inauguration of only the fourth Democrat governor in the history of the state.

Not only had my Republicans lost the governor's mansion in 1970, they also lost both Congressional seats. Years later I would chide my GOP brethren by saying, "I go away for one year to make the world safe for democracy, and you turn the whole state over to the Democrats?"

I don't remember much about my two weeks leave before I reported to California, except that I felt very out of place. I have heard it said that guys returning from World War II and Korea adapted much better upon their return because they had weeks at sea to decompress from war. I am not a psychologist; however, taking someone from a war zone and a day or so later depositing him back in his hometown is not a good idea.

It wasn't just the environmental shock of being in Vietnam one day and Mitchell, South Dakota, the next. It was the attitude of even my loved ones, and I don't mean this critically at all. However, it seemed that their feeling was, "Well, that's behind us; now let's all just go on like before."

Everyone just seemed to want to pretend as if it hadn't happened. Almost like the family had a nasty secret that they wanted to hide, like a bastard child. I am perhaps over dramatizing this; however, I know how I felt.

Quite frankly, later on, when anti-war people would confront me, it was almost better than this benign neglect I felt when coming home. At least the protestors acknowledged, if even in a negative way, my service.

Anyway, two weeks of this round-peg-in-a-square-hole ordeal and I was ready to head to California and my new assignment.

"WIZARD" OF VAN NUYS:

I mentioned earlier that an E-7 friend of mine in Vietnam knew the woman who made all 6th Army (West Coast) assignments and had wrangled me a California assignment, as I didn't want to spend my remaining few months in the army at some cold, winter duty station.

That place turned out to be a small Nike missile base in Van Nuys, California. As duty stations went, it had to be right up there with lifeguarding in Waikiki.

Probably not more than forty guys at the headquarters post on Victory Boulevard in the San Fernando Valley, and then some Nike launch sites up in the mountains surrounding L.A.

However, it wasn't just the amenities of a small post in sunny, southern California that made this so special; it was me and how I was treated and behaved during these last few months of my military career.

Although I have had a wonderful, fulfilling life, I have always pretty much had a second-fiddle role in things. I don't say that negatively or with resentment; it is just the facts.

In sports, I was always chosen about eighth in pick-up baseball and generally headed straight for right field without being told. Basketball, football, the same. In academics, always bottom quarter.

Even my political career, which started out great as I was elected South Dakota State Treasurer at age twenty-five, pretty well planed off after that, and my two races for Congress were disasters. To use a baseball analogy, I was a pretty good Triple A player who was never quite good enough for the "bigs."

However, in California, for a few brief months, I was Numero Uno. The boss of all I surveyed. The Wizard of Van Nuys. There were a number of factors that turned a Specialist Four from South Dakota into this major d'omo of a small Nike base.

First, I ran a one-man Public Information Office, a job that had not been filled in anyone's memory. I had my own office and absolutely nothing to live up to. I also discovered that the publisher of the Van Nuys newspaper was a former admiral in the navy and loved all things military.

In other words, any trite story or photos I took him got featured prominently in the local paper.

Which brings us to the colonel of this Camp Swampy on the Pacific, a very non-descript type whose only weakness was that he loved publicity. Quicker than you could say, "hold the presses," I had access to his car, driver and car phone (remember this was 1971). In other words, I once again had juice, and a lot of it.

To further enhance my persona, there was this Swedish girl in a Z car; however, out of deference to her I will skip that part of the story.

Finally—and most important to this process of turning an also-ran into a very important person—there was not another Vietnam veteran on base.

In fact, I had a sense that if you checked the background of a lot of the guys stationed there, you would have found an inordinate number of congressmen's relatives.

Now, it was about this time that the whole warped mystique of the Vietnam vet was being developed: The troubled—perhaps even psychotic—misfit, who might just lose it at anytime and end up going on some killing rampage.

For some time my fellow enlisted men looked at me rather strangely, as if trying to discern if I were capable of killing them all in their sleep some night.

While I was pretty screwed up mentally at this time anyway, I did everything I could to enhance this dark image of myself. I was very quiet, bordering on morose. I wore dark aviator sunglasses all the time and my hat low on my face. Then there was my uniform, with the dangerous-looking Screaming Eagle patch of my Vietnam division. All in all it was a hell of a show.

There were other incidents that even furthered this scary imagery. I remember once we were sitting around outside of our small Enlisted Men's Club and PX (post exchange). I was having a beer with a guy called Sparky, who was the colonel's driver and my Man Friday. Some other guys were seated nearby, talking about the upcoming Ali-Frazier heavyweight-boxing match. All of them were in total agreement that Ali would murder Frazier.

Finally, after listening to this for a while, I announced, "I will take all the bets that you want to make on Ali." They stared at me in stunned silence. While all of them would love to bet on Ali, they were not so sure they wanted to bet with this weird, scary Vietnam vet. So I announced again, "I mean it, I will cover all Ali bets. Just tell Sparky how much you want to wager." Then I walked off.

I have no idea what made me say it, as I quite frankly thought Ali would win also. However, it just seemed like the thing to do, and I don't recall that it involved a lot of money, as these guys threw nickels around as if they were manhole covers. Bottom line, however, Frazier upset Ali in that fight.

As they lined up to pay me off at the mess hall, they had a new respect for me, and I had a feeling that some of my fellow soldiers not only considered me a dangerous person, but one who was, in all probability, mobbed up; that I had somehow gotten inside information on the fight. How someone from South Dakota happened to become mobbed up I am sure never occurred to these guys.

Anyway, this brief period of being the head guy, both in terms of reality and mentally, was quite the time. In looking back at it over the past three decades, I can truthfully say it isn't a time I am very proud of.

I was plowing new ground here, and I am afraid I didn't do it very well. I found out I could be a bully—not an easy transformation for a guy who had always been bullied. I discovered scaring people had a dark satisfaction to it.

Also, the Swedish blonde in the Z car certainly did not distinguish me very well. Although there is a postscript there: When I was finally discharged, she took me to L.A. International, where there was this "Affair to Remember" kind of parting. Finally, as I was getting on the plane, I reached down and took off one of my medals and gave it to her. It was only after I was seated on the airplane that I realized I had given her my Good Conduct medal. Sometimes irony is too much.

It was a very mixed-up time for me, although I don't mean to use that as an excuse for bad behavior and not being a better person. In a way, it was like the other "Wizard of Oz" movie experiences I had throughout this adventure. At the end of that film, Dorothy pulls back the curtain and sees that the wizard is nothing more than a rather elderly gentleman pulling levers and turning dials.

She says to him, "You are a very bad man." To which he replies, "Oh no, my dear, I'm a very good man; I'm just a very bad wizard."

(I have used the "Wizard of Oz" analogy a good deal throughout this narrative because, in a way, it captures my army experience of being whisked up from a very mundane existence on the prairie and plopped down in the middle of a strange land among some very strange people and circumstances.)

EPILOGUE

There has been much written about how Vietnam vets were treated upon our return, and quite frankly I always thought a good deal of it was exaggerated. As I mentioned, I had a sense that a good many people just wanted to ignore or pretend we weren't there. Much like they wanted to ignore that horrible war.

I think the biggest problem I had was the number of people who wanted to argue about the war and just assumed that, as a Vietnam vet, I was pro-war. Nothing could have been farther from the truth. As I mentioned earlier, by 1970 all of us in Vietnam knew the war was lost.

However—and this is difficult to explain—it just didn't seem that someone who had not served had the right to criticize or demean the war or the sacrifices that others had made. I know that doesn't sound right, since everyone in this country has the right to oppose government policy, but it was how I felt. It just seemed as if people either wanted to ignore you or argue with you. I noticed this particularly when I traveled, and whenever possible I tried to avoid being identified as a Vietnam vet.

We had to wear our uniforms to fly military standby; however, once we got checked in at the airport we did not need the uniform. So I always carried a small bag with civilian clothes in it so I could go into a stall in the bathroom and take my uniform off.

One time I did not have the usual four-hour layover that involved flying standby, so I just kept the uniform on and went into the bar. I was standing off by myself when I heard someone next to me say, "You in Vietnam?" I thought, "Damn, here we go again." When I said I had been he put some money on the bar and said to the bartender, "Buy the soldier a beer." It would be the nicest thing anyone would do for me as a returning vet, until ten years later when we would dedicate the Vietnam Memorial.

I do not want to make any of this sound like a ploy for pity. Although when it happened I was somewhat bitter, I now realize it was just the times, the assassinations, political turmoil, misinformation from the government, and finally a war that seemed to have no end.

I had a sense that guys in uniform almost became a visible symbol for all of that, and somehow we became the object of people's anger and frustration. As misguided as that was, it has to be put into the context of the late 1960s and early '70s.

Getting out of the army would not be the end of my military experiences.

While I did not experience some of the more serious problems that plagued others, I nonetheless could not get comfortable being home.

In fact, one of the most difficult feelings I had to deal with was a strange desire to go back to Vietnam. Not out of some gung-ho, patriotic sense of the war, but more of a deep, indefinable desire to return. Like Zippo and Lucky, it was probably nothing more than adrenaline addiction. Also a nagging feeling that what I had been involved with in Vietnam made a difference to my friends there, and everything back home seemed so unimportant and mundane in comparison.

These feelings truly had me thinking I was cracking up, until I ran into another Vietnam vet one time in an airport and we started talking and I shared with him my thoughts and he told me he had the some desires. It really didn't solve anything; however, at least I knew I wasn't the only nut.

Like many Vietnam veterans, I would go through a divorce, which was epidemic among us—some estimates running as high as ninety percent. I have always felt one of the uncounted casualties of that war was this incredible toll on the marriages of returning vets.

I have no idea what caused this among my comrades; however, in my case it was my fault, and I have always felt that my ex-wife Susan deserved a lot better then she ever received from me.

However, not all my experiences after my service would be bad ones. I would have the privilege of serving in a program started by Ronald Reagan called Vietnam Veterans Leadership Program (VVLP), through which I met a wonderful group of veterans from across the country, many of whom remain my close friends today.

Reagan, by the way, became kind of a patron saint for us. We never had a VVLP meeting in D.C. that he did not invite us to the White House, and after all we had experienced, knowing the war was lost and yet having it insanely continue, it was wonderful to hear our commander in chief say, "I will never send American boys to fight in a war that the politicians do not have the guts to win." That statement, by the way, was very important to us because, in addition to whatever else we endured upon our return, we had a sense that veterans of other wars, especially World War II, looked down on us. That we were the guys who had lost "our war." This was especially true in the veterans clubs like the American Legion and Veterans of Foreign Wars (VFW), and was one of the reasons for establishing the Vietnam Veterans Leadership Program—so that Vietnam vets could find a support system outside of the established organizations. (We, of course, did not view the war as something we had "lost." In fact, I have a button that reads: "We were winning when I left."

Also, the notion of us "losing" the war was particularly galling given the realities of the conflict. Were it not for all the goofy rules of engagements, restrictions, and parameters that were placed on us, the war, for all intents and purposes, could have been over in a matter of months.

Where I was stationed at the Demilitarized Zone (DMZ), my division, the 101st Airborne Division, and the "Red Devils" of the 1st of the 5th Mech, who were stationed just north of us, could have been in Hanoi in a month if we had been turned loose.

All of that notwithstanding, everyone's vision of Vietnam will always be of us scurrying out of Vietnam, from the rooftop of our embassy, with our tails between our legs.

There was a horrible battle in World War I, at a place called Gallipoli in the Dardanelles, where British, Australian, and New Zealand troops were butchered on a wholesale basis. It was said of that battle: "Without victory, there is no glory, and there was no glory at Gallipoli." So too it was of Vietnam, regardless of the reason.

I have nothing but disdain for those who got us into this war and then placed all kinds of "one hand behind the back" limitations on us, and then—worst of all—continued the war for five years after they and everyone else knew it was lost. However, I have always had a loving respect for Ronald Reagan, who as president of the United States said that he was proud of us and appreciated our sacrifices.

I should add that while most Vietnam veterans had a deep reverence for Ronald Reagan, we also share a deep resentment for Jane Fonda. I know in recent years she has tried to do some historical revisionism and say she supported us but was against the war. Bullshit! That picture of her grinning on the North Vietnamese anti-aircraft gun with an NVA helmet on is one we will not forget.

A decade after returning, I would march in two parades, one in Chicago with my friends from VVLP, which was a great joy. I remember reading the paper the next day about a Vietnam vet in the crowd with his little boy. His son looks up at him and says, "It's a very long parade, Daddy." To which the father replies, "It was a very long war, Son."

However, my greatest experience would be the parade we had in Washington, D.C., to dedicate the Vietnam Memorial. We were lined up by states on the Mall, and it was a cold, raw day. My comrades and I figured, like most things where we were concerned, that this would involve just us and we would march down to the memorial by ourselves, which after ten years really didn't even bother us anymore.

We then began to move and pulled out onto Constitution Avenue and were absolutely shocked by the thousands of people lining the street cheering.

I cannot do justice to the incredible feeling we experienced by this outpouring of support and appreciation. I know I bawled the entire way down to the Vietnam Memorial site.

Here were all these wonderful people, who had come out on this cold day to cheer for us and hold up signs that said "Thanks" and "Welcome Home, Job Well Done" (this time we believed it).

As I said, I cannot do justice to this cathartic event, but it was as if we had been dipped in healing water. I just wish all of our Vietnam brothers and sisters could have been there with us that day.

I am sure my recollections of Vietnam are not entirely reflective of other soldiers who fought in that conflict. Because of its incredible length—over ten years—Vietnam was really a number of different wars that just happened to occur in the same place. First the advisors, then the professional soldiers who went over as a unit, then two-year draftees like me, who would show up years later in 1970.

However, the one common denominator we shared was the special dedication that we felt for each other, and still do to this day.

If you listen to veterans of any war, you will hear them talk about their close bonds to their fellow GIs, and perhaps it is true of any group that shared adversity and trying times together.

However, I think that was especially true of us as Vietnam veterans. I think that strong bond was forged because Vietnam was never a very popular war, and certainly by 1970 it seemed as if we were caught between the anti-war people at home and the enemy in Vietnam. That all we truly had was each other.

In the final analysis, I am glad I was drafted and served my country during that difficult time. Obviously, that is a much easier proposition because nothing bad happened to me. However, I think the whole military experience had a positive effect on me. Things had been pretty easy for me up to the point of my being drafted.

The army made me grow up and taught me about adversity. It taught me about dedication to others and loyalty. Also, it showed me that I was capable of doing much more and enduring much more than I would have ever thought possible. That knowledge—that I am capable of doing more—has helped me in other endeavors throughout my life. Sometimes I think I was at my best during the time I was in the military, and how very strange that seems, as the Army and war were certainly not what I would have ever sought out or wanted.

I have always been a student of our Civil War, and prior to my service in Vietnam could never understand how the soldiers in the Civil War could do what they did during that conflict. March for days on end, some with no shoes, little food, and then "dress right dress" and march with their comrades toward withering fire.

I think I understand it better now, and it has nothing to do with God, country, or some general in the rear. You suffer fatigue, fear, and all the other misfortunes of war because the guy next to you does it and the guy next to him, and you will not let them down or any of the others along that grim-faced line.

Anyway, it was one hell of a trip for a teacher from the plains, and like so many veterans' say, "I wouldn't go again but I would not trade the experience for anything." After my army adventures, I got back into politics. With my election as state treasurer in 1972, I became the youngest statewide elected official in South Dakota history. The voters re-elected me four times to a wonderful job that afforded me a chance to travel all over this great country and to other places around the globe. My political career included defeats as well as victories. I ran for Congress twice and got my head handed to me both times, but in both victory and defeat I came to love and respect the democratic process.

After leaving elective office, I entered the investment world—a job I hated. In 1995, I returned to South Dakota's capital city of Pierre for an eight-year stint in Governor Bill Janklow's cabinet. I then worked a short time as Janklow's statewide coordinator during his too brief Congressional career, which ended in 2004. Today, I am happily semi-retired and writing this tale.

As I finish these memories, of getting drafted and spending almost two years in the army, it is November 10, 2005. Tomorrow is Veteran's Day.

I began this by talking about how we have gotten much better at saying thanks to our young men and women who serve this country during times of war, and thank God we have. Even I, thirty-five years after serving in Vietnam, have people today who will say thanks when they learn I am veteran of that war. Last year, on Veteran's Day, I received three thank-you cards from friends, which is more than I had received in the previous three decades.

Tomorrow I will put on my 101st Airborne Division lapel pin and go to the Veteran's Day ceremony. I don't think of my fellow veterans as much as I should, especially those who died, and tomorrow is a good time to do that.

It is not an easy process, thinking about those young men of so long ago who were lost. Invariably, I see them as they would be today—getting gray and paunchy as they start to look forward to retirement, perhaps doting on and spoiling first grandchildren, or just enjoying a quieter and more sedate life that comes with maturity. God, what a horrible waste war is.

As I look back on this experience through the prism of time and remember the young men of all races, backgrounds, and personalities that I shared the army and the war with, I think perhaps Shakespeare captures my thoughts best, in the immortal lines of Henry V when addressing his troops before the battle of Agincourt in 1415:

> We few, we happy few, we band of brothers;
> For he today that sheds his blood with me
> Shall be my brother; be he ne'er so vile,
> This day shall gentle his condition:
> And gentlemen in England now a-bed

Shall think themselves accursed they were not here,
And hold their manhood's cheap whiles any speaks
That fought with us upon Saint Crispin's day.

Finally, I would like to say to the young men and women who currently wear the uniform of this country that thousands of veterans, from past times and past wars, stand with you. And that we are so very proud of you and so very thankful for your sacrifice.

Biography

Book

David Volk was born and raised in South Dakota. In 1969, after graduating from college, he was drafted into the US Army. He served two years in the Army — — —-a year of that in Vietnam. He served as a combat photographer with the 101st Airborne Division and was awarded the Army Commendation Medal and Bronze Star while in Vietnam.

In 1972, at the age of 25, he was elected State Treasurer of South Dakota, the youngest person in the state's history elected to statewide office. He was re-elected four times. He helped found and served as the first president of the National Association of State Treasurers.

He was appointed by the Reagan Administration as Chairman of the Vietnam Veteran's Volunteer Program for South Dakota, and was responsible for setting up an outreach program to troubled veterans from the Vietnam era.

He is a member of the American Legion, Veterans of Foreign Wars and Disabled American Veterans.

Made in the USA
Charleston, SC
13 March 2012